I AM
not amused

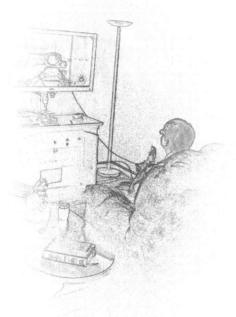

A Christian Response to
Media Entertainment

THOMAS MUROSKY, PH.D.

Our Walk In Christ Publishing
State College, PA

© 2019 by Thomas Murosky, Ph.D.

Published by Our Walk in Christ Publishing
State College, PA
www.owicpub.com

I AM Not Amused: A Christian Response to Media Entertainment

First Printing 2019
ISBN: 978-1-7325696-2-1 (sc)
ISBN: 978-1-7325696-3-8 (e)

The Internet addresses in this book are accurate at the time of publication. They are provided as a resource, but due to the nature of the Internet, those addresses may change.

Commitment to Open Source: Our Walk in Christ Publishing uses FOSS software where available. This book was produced with LibreOffice, GNU Image Manipulation Program, Sigil, Calibre, and the following open fonts: Charis SIL, Alpha Echo, Stardos Stencil, and DejaVu Sans. Chapter dividers obtained from https://openclipart.org. Audiobook edition produced with Audacity and Kid3.

LCCN: 2019931126

DEDICATION

This book is dedicated to Tyler G. I pray you will forever remember our conversations which led to the groundwork for writing this book. I also pray you will forever place these principles in your mind so you will not experience the depth of sin I had to endure. I wish you luck in your future endeavors and pray you always remember to seek God in all things.

ACKNOWLEDGMENTS

This book is the product of many years of being impacted by media in my own life, sermons and analysis from many pastors, and many conversations with several people about these principles.

First, for the early seeds of this work, Chip Ingram presented the message *Parenting in Perilous Times* which launched out my personal thought on these matters. Also, Stuart McAllister delivered his sermon *Media: Friend or Foe* which provided a lot of balance to my thoughts on entertainment, and finally Eric Holmberg, who produced *Hells Bells 2* and *Pandora's Box Office*. These productions showed the world I came from contrasted with the truth of God.

Next, I had some early discussions with my mentors David Hurd and Brett Vath who were a soundboard for proper entertainment once I became a Christian and began sanctifying my life.

To Tyler who had several years of conversations as he grew through adolescence into a young man. His conversations clarified more of my thoughts as they related to the next generation of people learning what it means to entertain themselves in the Internet age.

To Deb, Patrick, and once again Tyler for listening to most of the manuscript in the early form and providing feedback over that 10 day trip across country. Yep, that was a fun trip!

For the editorial process, thanks to Kate for her editorial comments and grammatical corrections and to Craig for also being a beta reader and discussing many of the finer points of the manuscript. Finally, thanks to pastor Reese for a few other notes of clarification and for beta reading the script.

CONTENTS

INTRODUCTION

Do you think movies are getting better for us to watch? a young teenager asked as we were riding the scrambler at DelGrosso's amusement park. Our conversations usually center on deep applications of scripture to our lives, as Jesus might call us to live as modern day Christians. Our studies were always so in-depth and the questions far beyond his age, and he was deeply concerned for the state of his soul during a period of life when many of his peers think only about pleasure, entertainment, and weekend breaks or summer vacations. I answered, "There are parts of media entertainment that are actually getting better, but parts are getting worse."

To explain further, we are in a time of democratization when Hollywood gives us what we want...but that means the producers give everyone what each entertainment category calls for. Our recent decade in film has begun to bring us thought-provoking Christian films while at the same time pushing the envelop of sin. As I write this, even Amazon is creating a movie where a pastor buys a prostitute to have a date for a church function, and he has to contend with falling in love with such a person. *Sausage Party* followed the same animation trends popular in many children's movies but the content was so vile it would have had an X rating only a short time ago, but alas it is openly available in the $3 movie bin at Walmart. Indeed, the answer to this question about whether movies are getting better or worse is not simple. As Christians, we need to examine our entertainment and make informed decisions about whether to watch specific films or play particular games.

I was glad my friend asked this question so early in our time at the park because the discussion of media entertainment and the modern Christian became the cornerstone of discussions on that unforgettable day. These conversations planted the seeds of this book and as they started to take root, I thought about how many kids hear about Jesus yet do not know how to apply Scripture to their entertainment. Given my experience with youth mentoring and the many struggles I encountered growing up in celluloid expansions, I wanted to write this book as a wake up call for modern believers to consider how Jesus would ask us to live in our democratized world of 'buy what you like'. I pray this book is a call to the individual, both old and young, but also to the church as a whole as we navigate the minefield that is media entertainment.

MY AMUSING JOURNEY

THE SHIFTING LANDSCAPE OF MEDIA ENTERTAINMENT

As I grew through adolescence into a young man, I watched as radical changes swept through all aspects of the entertainment industry. Cards and board games quickly took the back seat to the fast-paced, digital world of movies, television, music, and video games. I watched the rise and fall of the compact disk, and e-mail did not yet exist for the masses. Our movies were recorded on beta and VHS. LaserDisc was only in the imagination of the inventor waiting on the technology to arrive. DVD compression was discovered in my High School years and there was no Blue-Ray (can we please ignore whatever comes next?) I actually owned a Walk-Man branded device in which I could listen to cassette tapes on private headphones for the first time. I could get through three cassette tapes before my batteries died, and no, rechargeable batteries were not yet created for such devices. An amazing new technology arrived on the scene in my early High School days: a portable CD player. I could actually carry a hand-held CD player, though it would drain batteries before one full disc played to the end. MP3 compression technology promised to store many music CD's and I was an early adopter collecting my favorite tunes on a few small I-Omega Zip Disks in my college years. The shift progresses further.

The progressive technology is wonderful. As a Christian, I can load thousands of hours of solid preaching into a device that slides easily into my pocket in order to listen to God's Word any time I have a spare moment. I can access the entire Bible in every possible translation on my phone so I have no excuse to not read the Word. Excellent pastors utilize DVD technology for producing attractive, high-quality Bible studies while Social Media and free blogging platforms allow anyone to preach the Gospel or share Bible verses to be a blessing to those whom cares to see it. Despite the great applications, technology is actually neutral. While I can use these advances for great good, I can also utilize it for nefarious deeds. Vile images and video can be spread on the same model phone I use every day. It can be used to spread evil and deceit, laughter and jokes about sin, and let's not forget we can entertain ourselves to death by constant stimuli. As Christians, we may forget to study the word, pray, listen to sermons, or engage in Christian activity. In short, as Neil Postman said, we are *Amusing Ourselves to Death*.

I believe the evolution of technology has paved the way to our cultural affluence which in turn contributes to our amusing stupor. I was a child in the mid-1980's when we went outside in parks where friends gathered for a full day of outside play. Our parks were full of tag, board-games, and laughter. Our city supported local community parks each containing a game shack staffed by local teenagers. Us kids could borrow a board game for the afternoon and my personal favorite was the plastic ribbon used to weave bracelets.

The summer after we moved into the city, the *Nintendo Entertainment System* was released. The shacks were closed either from lack of budget or lack of use. The shack in our old park still stands, a ghost of the generations passed and probably lending itself to a ghost-story or urban legend the new neighborhood kids still tell. Trees have overrun our park, and the once-paved concrete foundation of the tennis and basketball courts are now subdued by a field of goldenrod and sumac. We kids abandoned the parks for our couches, first to play the great new video games, but also to watch more channels on cable television and see better, clearer images on newer movie technologies and larger screens. In short, we came inside to be amused instead by media entertainment.

I believe video games became the initial pull alluring us from the neighborhood yards and woods. We were awestruck by amazing new graphics and complexity of the games like *Zelda* and *Final Fantasy*. Prior to this time, the first video game system with replaceable game cartridges was the *Magnavox Odyssey*. This gaming system was first released in 1972 and had several versions and incarnations. Our neighbor had given us an Odyssey but we found it to be boring since it barely worked most of the time. Graphics and game play were similar to the *Atari* system that was more recognized because of the larger game selection coupled with the lower cost. Under 50 Bucks! The Atari system was more stable and the games were fun, but only for while. We could barely play the Atari for more than an hour so we kept on playing outside.

In the mid 1980's, *Nintendo Entertainment System* went on sale in the American market giving us comparatively excellent graphics and new complicated game play scenarios. The most popular game, *Super Mario Brothers*, took us about an hour to beat if you knew the game. In contrast, some games like *Final Fantasy*, *Zelda*, and *Metroid* contained complicated game play where the progress could be saved either by an onboard battery or a complicated passcode. The playtime of these games could take several hours to complete making them our games of choice for sleepovers or personal gaming missions. With these games came the advantage of holding our interest longer paving the way for longer and more complicated video games. The game play became so complicated that one person told me that since they purchased *Final Fantasy 11*, a third of his life had been taken up without even finishing the game (this was shortly after the game was released in the early 2000's).

Nintendo became embroiled in a gaming war between several companies in competition to produce better graphics and more complicated sequences. Most of the industry was finding ways to sell sex and violence that was trying to find expression in our modern times, titillating our natural sin (I will note also that the Nintendo corporation has always produced the most family-friendly games). While NES utilized 8 bit graphics, the *Sega Genesis* countered with 16 bit graphics. The companies fought their way out of bit-range entirely until the top consoles to date, *Xbox* and *PlayStation* brands, have graphics that could easily be movies. While the Nintendo could design a crudely drawn 'potion', now main-stream video games sport the full range of graphic content including incorporating clear marketing labels from well-known companies. In short, anything can now be incorporated into a video game including actual animations filmed and cut in movie studios. The games seem no longer to be games, but an extension of our very lives, a truth well elucidated by the creation of *Second Life* and *World of Warcraft*.

The video games and industry have many positive attributes, though the negatives should also be weighed. As a child, we played games as our new way of socializing. It was not the exercise we received while playing outside, but the way a group of friends could play, laugh, and even stay out of trouble. As an adult mentoring youth, I have experimented with video games in my mentoring and one of my most memorable weekends with a teenager was playing some of the modern military games. On the negative side, however, video games can be a source of addiction in our lives and the lives of our children. Though it can be fun to play some video games, the best thing to do is limit the playing to a short duration, and even eliminate them entirely most days. This target has become more difficult to achieve due to the increasing complexity in modern games and the limited ability to save on the spot. As Christians, we need to examine the content of the game in addition to the potential to cause addiction or excessive game play for ourselves and our families.

Though I believe video gaming drove the kids inside, I think television programming added more screen addiction to our lives while capturing our minds all the more. I did not watch a lot of television as a kid, mostly because we did not have cable and our antenna would only pick up a few fuzzy stations. I do have fond family memories of watching *Unsolved Mysteries* when we moved to a new town closer to a broadcasting city. Shortly after that move, we hooked up cable TV precipitating an increase in my television viewing. A few years later in 1997 I stopped watching television all together and I do not miss it. During my college and graduate school years, I only caught a few shows at someone's house, though I often played some familiar movies from my personal collection simply for background noise. When I returned to watching more television with a young man that I mentored 15 years later, I was absolutely shocked at a few differences in how programming worked.

My first observation was the ability to watch the same program repeated over and over on a given channel. All I had to do was find the station out of 500 or so available that ran the program on loop and I could, 'turn on, tune in, and drop out' of reality. Before I knew it, several hours had passed and I was not even at my house! This approach was born in the marketing minds of pure democratic choice in what we watch as Americans. Want 24/7 golf? We got it! A non-stop hack and slash horror channel? I have not looked, but I am sure it is out there somewhere. Whatever is wanted by a paying customer can be accommodated by the industry to make the sale.

My next observation was the shift in the main actor to be the story teller and the salesman as I saw the him in the program and again on the commercials. Since we are already watching only the shows we want to watch, the characters who can sell us the story can certainly convince us to purchase the sponsor's product. Considering the programming is established and the products are setup to sell, the actor is not only our storyteller, but also our product guide to sell us the solutions to all of our problems.

My final observation was a shift in the commercial placements. Various commercials are still placed in the middle of the program between suspenseful moments, but additional commercial breaks are frequently added just before the end of the program. Long ago, the program would end and the credits would roll, then a commercial break before the next show started. Now the programmers give us the new commercial break just before the end sequence and then immediately start the next program as the credits roll on the previous show. This basically ensures the programmers they have a captive viewer to sit by for another episode even despite the intention to turn off the television after 'this' show ends. So combined together, these shifts have increased the addictive nature of television to better hold captive the audience and sell more products. It is a wonder we get up to buy things at all, but of course we can buy things without getting up from our television sets!

Just as video games and television shifted over the years, the same is true for movies. The obvious shift has been an increase in special effects starting with the amazing computerized effects in the 1991 *Terminator 2, Judgment Day*. This film debuted in my young teenage years letting us experience the shift from clay animation to computerized graphics. Shortly after, Pixar supplanted hand-drawn animations of the cartoons in my past. More than just visual differences, I also observed the lengthening of films and the spawning of many more genres opening the way not only for more gruesome horror and full-length movie documentaries, but also the creation of high-quality Christian films.

I enjoyed my childhood movies, but as newer films peaked my interests, I temporarily forgot the films of my past. I later went back to many early favorites to observe content that was hardly suitable for my young eyes. The kids in those films cussed and displayed horrible behavior. Sexual references were all throughout the movies in the 1980's as producers and directors sought to break every taboo and meanwhile the people just bought the films that pleased

> We contributed to the problem by brushing the objectionable matter under the mat of a wonderful story.

them, choosing to brush the objectionable matter under the mat of a wonderful story. This led to our Christian habit of letting pleasure become our standard for orthodoxy. Since this time, however, I have noticed 'family-friendly' movies have actually improved in content.

My second observation about how movies have changed over time is called **democratization**. This term means that the paying audience guides the availability of the product, in this case, the movie. Democratization on the positive led to the creation of the Christian movie market and helped in cleaning up family-friendly films while maintaining a place for the alternative films other people are still interested in buying. On the negative, democratization is also why the pornography industry will never die since people will spend money to buy images that titillate their pleasures.

Movie length has also seemed to shift over time[i]. Movies back in the 1980's tended to be around 90-100 minutes long for the average movie we watched, but through the mid 1990's, that started to shift to about 2 hours. During the 2000's, a few movies, notably *Lord of the Rings* started to have even longer versions and then releasing extended-play editions to the retail market. With the sales proving America likes longer films, *Harry Potter* split the last movie into two movies setting a trend for *Twilight, Hunger Games,* and *The Hobbit.* Indeed, the average length of movies has increased almost an hour which is over 40% increase in time all the while saying that the 'attention span' of children is declining. I suggest we do not have an attention span problem in America - we have a media-saturation problem and until we address the addiction of over stimulation, our culture will continue to decline. Our increased movie length and greater time spent playing games is evidence our attention spans are not shorter, we simply do not want to let go of the entertainment in order to expand our minds.

Our distraction by movies, television, and video games removed our attention from work to focus on our next pleasure, but, a new creation was brewing in the later 1990's that would dominate all these sources of media. The Internet was making an appearance, crudely at first, then with a power to dominate the market. Just like cable television and a phone in the 1990's, it is uncommon for people not to have an Internet connection today. I was part of the last generation growing up without being perpetually connected to the whole world. We neither had

---

[i]There is a difference between the averages I report here and the averages found on Wikipedia and other online resources. When I looked into the matter of movie averages over the years, it does seem they are reported as mostly not changing, however, the movies used as examples of average length were not movies that I have ever heard of. When balancing the movies that were both successful and those we actually watched in my youth, the movies of the 80's and 90's were shorter in duration than similarly popular movies as the decades proceeded.

computers nor personal phones and we survived; better for it in the end. But now we have 24/7 access to fast-paced information that has the power to distract us or make us wealthy if only we could tame the beast within ourselves. Like other great technologies, the Internet is a neutral place where people can express their heart. They will use the Internet for great good or for great evil, but rarely anything in between. Ravi Zacharias said it well that improved technology merely gives us an improved means to reach our deteriorating ends. At the root of that statement lay our inherent sin and so we are prone to use this great tool for evil deeds. I will add that with self-control we can also usher this awesome tool for amazing good and grow closer to the Lord with the powerful, digital sword that is the Word of God.

MY EARLY ENTERTAINMENT

My brother and I experienced the latch-key kid life before that term was coined. My brother left our apartment in the morning to ride the bus to the local elementary school. Once he left, I was to go to the sitter's house in direct sight of our apartment. My Kindergarten years began as such because my mother and step father worked early, leaving before we awoke. Those mornings give me cherished memories of watching *Kids Corporation* and the first ever season of *Transformers*. I enjoyed *He-man* later that afternoon and I must also confess my early love for *Care Bears*. Michael Jackson recently released *Thriller* featuring the song *Beat It*, my favorite during my early life. The expansion of cable television opened the door for MTV to provide a place to mainstream the production of music videos and the Home Box Office provided a way to watch movies at home without purchasing expensive equipment. At our apartment, we only watched the programming made available by our rabbit ear antenna. In those days, parents could truly monitor their kid's choice in entertainment, and the programming entering the house generally provided decent morals for society that had not yet fully slipped into post-modern moral relativism where anything is permissible in the marketplace.

Near the end of Kindergarten, we moved to another state when our parents split up. I became a single mother's son when young kids generally played outside, rarely listened to music, and did not have unlimited access to video games. During this very important time in my life, the American culture began refining its focus on entertainment of all varieties. Cable television began its sprawl across the country, video games decreased in price so the average family could afford them. "Under 50 Bucks!" was on the lips of kids begging for the Atari system. Nintendo prepared to release its first cartridge video game system, and it launched in the American market for a pricey $299. My brother and I received our Nintendo in the second Christmas season after the price dropped, but our neighbors received their Nintendo for Christmas the year it came out, increasing our covetous desire for our own gaming system. Their family always acquired the latest technologies and toys right when they arrived on the market, giving us somewhere to hang out and learn about the new inventions.

About this time, my mother's co-worker purchased a cable TV package including several movie channels. Our recent acquisition of a VCR allowed us to record some television programs and rent movies, but now for only the cost of blank videotapes, we could own several movies. In this arrangement, we would be given the programming menu at the beginning of the month and we circled the movies we wanted recorded. My brother and I each picked out a few movies from the catalog and she would then record those movies onto the tapes for delivery to my mother when they were all recorded. We took great privilege to acquire movies we previously watched and liked, or maybe a few that just seemed interesting. I cannot recall being told 'No' to any movie in this arrangement, so I had acquired a collection of *Friday the 13th*, *Nightmare on Elm Street, Stand By Me*, and several other R rated movies of the day. Though I did have access to these 'R' rated films as a young boy, in those times our parents still limited our television time so the negative impact did not manifest itself in our lives until later when supervision was relaxed.

As our culture began the trends toward entertainment we, too, were caught up in the movement centering our lives around the television instead of spending our time outside. The progression was made complete when we moved to a new town shortly before my 10th birthday. Our VHS movie collection grew allowing us more time viewing our favorite movies and our Nintendo received regular game-play. About a year after moving into this new house, we also hooked up cable television. While we played in the woods a lot as kids, we all but forgot about the woods near the new house. Though we knew every inch of the forest in the old city, the new forest remained a mystery while the stories of our times were being unfolded daily before our eyes.

The arrival of music to my ears completed my submersion into media entertainment. My brother's music secretly became my own taste. This was a fact I was not anxious to reveal to anyone. Prior to this time, I heard music on the radio, though I never gave it the time of day to think about. I started as young as eight with Weird Al, but shifted to Def Leppard, Mötley Crüe, and a few years later, Megadeth and Metallica. In High School, my tastes shifted again as I moved to the lighter sounds of Pink Floyd and Rush. Like many teenagers, music played a large part in my life as I struggled through challenges seemingly alone. It was the sounds of music that acted as a back-drop soundtrack to my miserable life.

Looking back, we were the generation that lived through the radical changes which moved entertainment to the central focus of life. We are constantly entertained now, even during work. It has become, at its root, an addiction. Whether it is a movie, during the off-times, music playing in the background, or a free video game on our phones, we turn to entertainment as a way to pass the small seconds we used to spend in thought. It has progressed so far that even walking the isles in grocery stores I observe more people wearing headphones than not; stupefying themselves in their own world while out shopping. Whether this is a good trend or a bad, I will leave my readers to their own opinions.

EARLY CORRUPTION

Media entertainment as a broad category is neutral, though individual flavors of entertainment are open to subjective opinion. Some people will argue that mature audiences can watch almost anything but kids should be shielded from some programming. I personally, based on experience, believe elements of this thought-process are true though I would draw lines in very different places for reasons we will discuss later in this book. I was deeply corrupted by my horrible entertainment, though it took some time for such personal putrefaction to manifest itself in my life. Corruption set in, polluting my heart, my mind, and my life. The impact was not just short-lived, but lasted well into adulthood, effecting me even today. So wisdom may be imparted, I implore my readers to learn from my missteps for themselves and their families.

In my first grade year, my mom and brother would go to the weekly cub scout meeting. I stayed home alone every week developing the ritual of watching (or rather listening) to the movie *Stand By Me* while I played with my Micromachines. *Stand By Me* features a group of extremely foul-mouthed pre-teen kids who make up a story about staying at each other's houses as a cover up to spending the weekend walking the rail-road lines in search of a dead body. I love the movie, and if it did not contain an endless stream of vulgarity, I would probably watch it again. Do not get me wrong, I am not a prude, nor do I believe that the 'F' word will send a person to hell, but my focus is on the attitude behind the words. When a character in a film or a vocalist in a band inputs into us an endless stream of vulgarity, we will certainly be impacted by the attitude behind the words. As our attitude declines, we will start to display ingratitude resulting in a lower view of the world, and therefore we will make a less positive impact on the people around us.

I learned a powerful, yet terrifying imagery lesson during these formative years. Limiting time with negative imagery never removes images out of our heads. At a visit to our neighbors house during the summer between 2nd and 3rd grade, the kids told us they found their dads movies and put one in. Confused about the content, I watched my first X-rated pornography film that day. The images are still in my head, refusing to leave, refusing to die, just waiting for an opportunity to fester should I give them an inch. This lesson is not exclusive to pornography, though that is a poignant example. In reality, all our media choices leave the same imagery branded in our minds, forever polluting, forever corrupting, forever waiting for expression in our hearts, thoughts, and actions. It is not just the case with movies, but transfers also to music, games, and the Internet. Had I learned the actual lesson of branding imagery in those early years of my life, it may have saved me many more struggles during my young development.

To further the decay, I progressively began viewing horror, hack and slash, and similar movies. Senseless murders, acts of sex and sexual perversion became infused in my young mind more so then any of my peers. The impact on my mind became difficult to ignore. My 5th grade creative writing assignment first began to demonstrate the negative effect my entertainment imposed on my own thinking. I was not watching many of the traditional kid's films of my day, but I knew every word out of the mouth of Freddy Kruger. The hack and slash influence came pouring out of my mind when we were assigned to give ten reasons why our parents did not sign our homework paper. I wrote down that Freddy Kruger killed my mom, and Jason Voorhees cut up my mom with an ax. I also indicated things like she went parachuting and the chute didn't open. Just like the child of an alcoholic does not know that his family is dysfunctional, I did not realize these answers were inappropriate. Stuart McAllister says that our modern conversations are an overflow of our media diet. Psychologists suggest how we grow up, for better or for worse, is what we consider 'normal'. When the teacher called my mom with the report on this homework assignment, I was grounded from my horror movies for an unspecified amount of time. That only lasted until I received my copy of *Friday the 13th Part 7* a few days later.

A battle raged silently in my heart, but the manifestation of the filthy entertainment had not yet boiled over in my public life. My loud and dark music choices became an outward reflection of this struggle. I focused on the depressing songs comforting me as I wallowed in my own depression. The dark music solidified my friendships with the wrong crowd in school leading to problems with the law in 7th grade, being offered drugs in 8th grade, and almost failing that year due to a focus on friends and pleasure. Other songs struck a chord in my heart because of the meanings, some for their provocative nature, and others for the beat. Some of these songs contained harmless messages, but others boasted dangerous themes. The rock stars became our idols and shaped our minds.

My High School music taste included a broad spectrum of everything from classical music to gangsta rap. Though I loved the beat and even the struggle detailed in some rap, the vulgar words started to flow from my mouth. At 16, a friend and I decided not to swear because we viewed vulgarity as a sign of lower education. After only two years of listening to rap, my mouth wove a tapestry of profanity that would make a truck-driving sailor blush! I think that some of this had to do with the horrible life circumstances of my late teenage years, but I certainly credit much of this to my choices in music.

Please understand this is not about the external behavior. Our inner attitude is at stake here, but the words that come out of our mouth are often a reflection of our own heart. A poor heart leads to poor service rendered to human-kind. If we can show the corrupting power media manifests in our hearts, does it not make sense to filter out the negative messages so we can better our friends and neighbors? I wager a good heart is more important than entertainment, especially since clean entertainment which does not soil our hearts is also available.

MEDIA'S POSITIVE IMPACT

Media can relate to us as we navigate life. While our struggles brew to full-scale assault on our emotions, the music that creates the soundtrack of our lives mirrors our thoughts and feelings. If we analyze the music that resonates with our heart, we can learn what we may become. While the music, at first, may appear to be destroying us we may begin to realize it could just be a mirror reflecting our own inclinations. It can direct and lead our lives as well, but to be honest in a book about the impact of media entertainment in our life, I must also show how music and movies helped me in the darkest times of my life, as it likely does with many other people.

Our house became a total party scene, at least where small-scale high school parties were concerned. While I remained a recluse in the sanctuary of my bedroom, my brother was a social savant inviting friends over in the summer nights when my mother worked third shift. Our home became the place where the hoodlums gathered for their first sexual experiences while experimenting with drugs and this occurrence made my personal temptations to engage in these teenage revelries even greater than many of my peers. Many nights left me stranded in my bedroom because opening the door subjected my lungs to a smokescreen. Cigarette and illegal drug smoke routinely covered the top five feet of the ceilings. It was music that made my sanctuary a bearable place to be.

Music was not just a refrain from the stress of life since I also credit my music as giving me the final confirmation that I needed to refrain from experimenting with drugs myself. My brother decided to trip on acid for the first time on a summer night. He made a connection to a dealer whom was invited over. This guy shattered all of the stereotypes our school taught us about drug dealers. Rather than a scraggly, dirty man, this guy was dressed for success. I had not ever seen someone so slickly dressed and to look him over, I would never suspect him of being engaged in such a business. He sat down at our kitchen table and promptly reached into the right inner pocket of his leather jacket for his bag of acid and into the left for a 9mm handgun. That, to me, was the perfect recipe for an interesting evening!

Beyond initial impressions, this dealer was also one of the nicest people that I ever met. We talked a lot about music, and he even introduced me to the band *Rush* which quickly became a favorite in my high school years. After our initial chit-chat about music and such, the conversation switched over to the drugs. I had no interest in using acid on the basis that I thought drugs were stupid. He asked me if I would like to try it, but I said no. Unlike many other drug pushers I have known up to that point, he was very nice about it saying, "OK, if you change your mind, let me know!" That night was the closest I ever came to using drugs, but I keenly watched the unfolding events of that night.

My brother was instructed on how to use the paper and they began the trip. I did not immediately seek my usual refuge, but rather became interested in the things they were 'seeing', and the 'fun' they appeared to be having. I finally secluded myself in my room with a struggle on my mind. I was thinking of trying this drug to see what it was like. After all, no one has yet died tonight of these drugs and everyone seemed to be having fun, well, everyone but me. I pondered these things, weighing the truth of the matter, and even wondering if truth was really knowable. I played *The Wall* by Pink Floyd through my headphones and thought about this struggle. The fifth song echoed in my ears and the chorus of children sang, "We don't need no education; we don't need no thought control". The music helped me to see the bigger picture on the horizon. I would not be using the drugs for my future. I desired to raise children some day and I wanted to be able to tell them that I had not used any drugs even in the most difficult of circumstances. I wanted them to know that it is possible to navigate life in general and High School in particular without using drugs. Music helped me to see all that.

My new resolve allowed me to see what everyone was doing without the temptation. I left my room to discover a dark house, and I thought they might have left, except the truck was still in the driveway. As I approached the black living room, a sudden shriek and a quiet shiver emanated from the corner. A body lay hiding under a blanket. My eyes adjusted to the dark as I barely made out each person in their own mental prison. The fun had passed and the nightmare had begun. The acid was now hitting their mind with such force that they sought to escape the sounds and visions. They were stuck cowering in the corner, afraid of the world, running away in terror. This concluding scene in the darkness sparked infinite gladness that I had decided not to participate in the evening's 'fun'. It was Pink Floyd that saved my life that night, particularly ironic since they are not exactly pharmaceutical prohibitionists.

This example is certainly one outlier describing how music is important for any generation coping with dreary landscapes of adolescence, but it is not limited to that life stage. I could easily tell of the stories where music, movies, and games bring us closer together as people as we share experiences. These forms of entertainment serve a very real purpose in our life, but it is a purpose that is so deep we absolutely must understand it; and if we are Christians, we must ask what God would think of the things that we use to entertain ourselves.

PURIFYING THE CHRISTIAN

Many believers, particularly those that come to Christ later in life, have an incubation period before they really start to behave like Christians. The length of this period depends on how long a new believer has been going to church before becoming a Christian, lifestyle choices before becoming a Christian, time reading or knowledge of the Bible, and remorse over the past. My incubation period lasted about 3 years. During this time, my outward life started to look a little cleaner, though, mostly I looked like the rest of the world in my entertainment. Some of my friends and other influences also looked similar to the world, but after reading the Bible a couple of times and attending church services for a few years, I started to learn in depth about my faith. My life was becoming on track with what the Apostles wrote about in their letters I was setting aside the old 'Gentile' thinking and replacing those thoughts with the glorious thoughts of God.

We never know what will be the catalyst to seriously move our life in alignment with Christ. It might be a friendship or a sermon. Perhaps a good movie or song. I know during an early stage of cleaning up my old life, I heard a sermon that caused me to place God at the center of my entertainment. The pastor at a church service talked about King Josiah and how he came to purify Israel. The book of the law had been lost through generations of idolatry, but was later discovered during a command from the king to clean the temple. The Law was brought to the king, and as he read the words he tore his clothes in repentance realizing his nation had not been following God's commands as they were written. Josiah cast out the temple prostitutes, cut down the poles and destroyed the pagan alters. In short, he abolished the worship of false gods but also removed the means the people had used to worship those gods. I realized upon reflection I needed to do the same, not with the pagan ways, but with the entertainment; or perhaps the idol worship is really the same.

I took inventory of my music and movies, computer files and games. Since I read the Bible a few times during this inventory, I quickly assessed what entertainment was aligned with God and that which was not. My question was simple: how does my entertainment compare with the Word? Any entertainment crossing my eyes underwent critical examination under the microscope of God's Word, and so it should be! My examination demonstrated that some of my entertainment was good or neutral, but some needed to be purged from my life. I attempted to sell anything I determined should be removed from my collection. I allotted a few weeks for sale of CD's but a lot of perfectly good discs went into the trash can. Some VHS tapes also needed to go, so I actually took a hammer and destroyed some tapes to the vision of Josiah cutting down the Asherah Poles. My computer files consisting of a few *Family Guy* and *South Park* episodes in addition to some stand-up comedians, all got the trash can. I had no more need for such filthy entertainment, I had Christ at the center, and entertainment does not need to be full of crude or sexual humor.

Now with my purification on way, I wanted to monitor the entertainment further entering my house. This monitoring task was easy during the next few years on account of limited funds. My true challenge began a few years later when I began to have some disposable income, but with Christ as my central focus, I was able to keep a firm grasp on my goal.

Some people will no doubt view such regulation on entertainment as legalistic, but I want to echo what Chip Ingram frequently says, "Maybe I am just being Holy". God does command us to examine everything carefully, hold fast to that which is good and abstain from every evil thing (*1 Thessalonians 5:21-22*). Why do we want to make an exception for what we watch or what we play or what we listen to? Why do we think that entertaining ourselves with media that glorifies or makes humor out of sin is a good thing? Our savior died for such sins, and we look upon them to laugh and be amused. Perhaps it is not being legalistic to try to be holy.

RECONTAMINATED

My sanctification has slipped over the years. A couple of years ago I looked at my growing collection of DVD's to see movies not representative of what Christians should watch. I was caught off guard without thinking about it, my filter broke and let filth into my house. My television was once a small, old device used once or twice a month to watch a movie or more frequently a sermon on DVD. This small television was replaced by a large-screen model. It moved from a small corner in the office to the center piece of the living room. I did not have cable TV, but I did increase the time watching movies or playing video games, primarily while mentoring a group of teenagers. The fellowship factor certainly played a role in bringing the television back to the center of the house, but the problem began when the device grabbed my personal time as well. I do not regret the increase in the television size or the new placement in the general living area, just the larger amount of time it was before me and the types of movies accumulating. I needed a re-examination of my commitment to remove the filth from my house.

I do not regret the slip since I was able to influence many teens for the positive around that television, but the problem occurred when I started buying more movies without consciously examining my purchases. I did not buy movies full of filth, but I noticed a few old horror films appearing in my collection, probably for "old times' sake". Once I made the realization that my sanctification was slipping in my personal life, I acted quickly to purge those films sparking my decline. I realized I was re-contaminated. My time in front of the television increased, my time in the Word and in other helpful books had decreased, my prayer life had suffered. In short, I started to revert back to who I was before becoming a Christian. That was not good, so I needed to go back through my life again, change around what I was doing, and figure out how to come back to Christ with this new realization.

We all need a reboot, maintenance, or course correction from time to time. It is not something to be ashamed of, just something we do. We frequently need to re-evaluate our diet and exercise, our time with families and work, our commitments and plans. How is our time with Christ any different? We get excited about God and read our Bibles a lot, then it gets boring and we slow down and before we know it, our precious book is collecting dust in the corner. The balance to this trend is found in the Old Testament annual feasts. Once a year, Israelites would go to the designated place to offer sacrifices to God and to recommit their lives to Him. We should do that as well, as often as we can. Annually is good, but monthly is better. We should devote ourselves to a day to spend in worship to Him, we should try to memorize scripture, pray, and attempt to get through the Bible at least once a year. Resist contamination by recommitting to God.

Chapter Questions

1. What tech changes have you seen in media entertainment? Overall, are they good, bad, or neutral changes?

2. What is democratization? How has this trend changed media entertainment?

3. What determines your standard for entertainment?

4. Do you agree kids have lower attention spans? Why or why not?

5. Think about your journey through entertainment. How has it affected you?

6. When did you become a Christian? How long did it take you to conform your life to Christ?

7. Do you feel that your entertainment would please Christ right now? What changes might you make today?

2

WRITING THE BALLADS

If a man were permitted to make all the ballads he need
not care who should make the laws of a nation
- Andrew Fletcher

As we venture through our examination of media entertainment, it is important to consider what the artists themselves say about their creations. It seems media's proponents and opponents always cross words, both making specific claims about the entertainment they produce. Truly, what is the intended meaning behind a song, a movie, or a game? Do artists really just create entertainment for creation's sake? We cannot rule out some art is constructed to teach or promote a concept or a lifestyle. Education was the intention behind the after school HBO presentation, *The Truth about Alex,* and another program by CBS titled *What if I'm Gay?* Both of these presentations were produced as after school specials to entertain but also to teach kids about homosexuality as merely another lifestyle choice. While our modern culture routinely discusses homosexuality, the 1980's media landscape generally treated the topic as taboo. Like all social agendas, artists broke into media to influence the audience's mind, which slowly becomes law. To that end, the next two chapters will examine how media affects us and what the modern artists intend to teach the consumers through their art, whether present or absent from the life of Christ. With the popular artist's influence established, we will determine what they intend to teach us and what lifestyle has resulted from their beliefs.

Early World Entertainment

On the seventh day of creation, God rested, and the command to observe the Sabbath was included in the ten commandments to reflect the general principle of rest from a hard week's work. The exact purpose of the Sabbath is not entirely clear. It could have been a day to set aside for the complete worship of God, or it could have been a day set aside to merely rest. Because the entire Israelite social system was theocratic and Paul declared Jesus the fulfillment of the Sabbath rest, its observance was no longer commanded according to a few separate verses from Pauline writings (*Romans 14:5, Colossians 2:16*). I will simply suggest our rest is a matter of the conscience and I will leave the discussion of the Sabbath intent to others. With that, however, we are free to engage in entertainment to the extent God is honored by what we do.

We know that the root of the Olympics was born from the sports-like competitions used to showcase the best warriors of the ancient Greece. Gladiatorial games were spawned by the cruel Emperor Nero who turned the games from simple competitions into a bloody fight to the death. Sin had taken hold and our bloodlust spilled over into violence. The gladiatorial games finally ended when a martyr named Telemachus died in the arena in protest to Christian Rome participating in the ungodly games[1]. His death ended the gladiatorial games once and for all under Emperor Honorius, but we know what comes next for our unrestrained entertainment: either more bloody violence, uncontrolled heathen sex, or maybe a spattering of other sin.

The lost city of Pompeii was discovered in the mid 1700's and the archaeological excavation continues today. The archaeologists revealed a culture so vile the people experienced what had to be a replay of Sodom and Gomorrah. Curiously, another town, Herculaneum, was also destroyed by the same volcano, Mount Vesuvius, in AD 79. The still available artwork inscribed on the statues, pillars, and walls in these towns depict a city totally saturated in sex and perversion. I am not about to suggest all natural disasters in our world are God's specific judgment, but perhaps artwork from the valley of salt would yield similar imagery before the sulfur fell from the skies, and perhaps God acted in this manner to destroy a city so vile a message would ring through to the young expanding church: beware of resting too comfortably, a lesson Israel failed to learn time and again through the historical period of the judges. About the great city of Pompeii, the artist Bastille wrote[2]:

> Oh where do we begin?
> The rubble or our sins?

This artist asks a reasonable question which we must ask ourselves. Though our world is mostly not in total rubble, the sin of the culture is leaving a rubble of wrecked lives, ruined marriages, fatherless children, and drug and alcohol abuse. Do we start with our rubble or our sin? That is the core of what we are trying to answer in this book.

Pleasure is entertainment's destination, and research has shown the more affluent a culture becomes, the greater the people seek both pleasure and entertainment. Since all means of entertainment is from the hearts of the people that produce it, it is not any wonder that their heart comes out in the art they produce. C.S. Lewis wrote the great series *The Chronicles of Narnia*. Though people frequently say that he wrote it to portray the sacrifice and redemption of Christ, that is simply not true. C.S. Lewis spoke many times on the subject and made it very clear he was merely writing in-depth children's stories during a time it was assumed people did not want to read fanciful tales (an aspect he made light of in Eustace's family in *The Voyage of the Dawn Treader*). He says that the Christ-like imagery merely came out of his heart because defending Christianity was one of the ultimate callings in his writing. But some hearts are full of evil. During the creative process, the evil present in an artist's heart will spill out into the books, games, and productions they create and the end result will be a work that is not wonderful or beautiful, but twisted and evil. Such was the case of the *Golden Compass* series. The author, Philip Pullman, is an outspoken atheist. His childrens' story depicted an enemy who was none other than God Himself. Such was the outpouring of his heart. In light of this, one Christian commentator of the entertainment industry revealed that for the most part, the writers, directors, and producers in Hollywood are generally not church-going people, and do not typically regard God or His word. Let us not be mistaken, if these are the people that are writing the shows we watch, let us not presume their views on life will not impact our own worldview. My message is clear: be careful what you watch on your television, do on your computer, or listen to in your personal time while secluding yourself through headphones.

Considering some artists teach out of intention and others teach out of the overflow in their hearts, we are led to a discussion of ethics. Most college programs now require students to take ethics courses. I was a graduate student studying biological sciences and our ethics course was intended to teach about what is right and wrong in scientific studies. Of course, the typical university preaches there is no absolute truth, so how can we possibly define what is 'right' and what is 'wrong' in a college ethics course? This is not a moot point because when the ground was broken for the USC film school, the attendants were Steven Spielberg, George Lucus, Irvin Kershner, and Randal Kleiser. In the article about the event, Lucas gave this ominous observation of the position of film in our modern age:

> Film and visual entertainment are a pervasively important part of our culture, an extremely significant influence on the way our society operates. People in the film industry don't want to accept the responsibility that they had a hand in the way the world is loused up. But, for better or worse, the influence of the church, which used to be all-powerful, has been usurped by film. Films and television tell us the way we connect our lives, what is right and wrong.[3]

From one of the top directors of that time, and even still currently after three decades, Lucas reminds us that film and television do impact our lifestyle and thought. He even acknowledges movies and television impact us more than the church, for better or for worse. For this reason, Lucas goes on:

> It's important that the people who make films have ethics classes, philosophy classes, history classes. Otherwise we are witch doctors.[4]

It is interesting Lucas wants to talk about ethics. According to *Webster*, ethics is the area of study dealing with moral right and wrong. From sciences to business, to human and animal studies, universities that proclaim there is no moral right and wrong want to teach their students about what is right and wrong! Chip Ingram deals with this problem in his message on *Whatever happened to Right and Wrong?*[5] He says that everyone agrees we need ethics, but no one can agree on whose ethics we adopt. I agree. My ethics, my moral rights and wrongs, are defined by God's character as expressed in His Word. Other people say we should let our internal compass and feelings define what is right 'for us'. This was the message in an interview with John Lennon and Yoko Ono who helped to spread the mantra of existentialism, which is basically the 'do your own thing' philosophy. Ravi Zaccharius, however, observes that some cultures want to eat with their neighbors while other cultures want to eat their neighbors...do we have a preference? Yes, ethics are important, but unless those ethics are grounded in truth, they may be little more than lip service. We will continue a discussion of Christian ethics in chapter 4, for now, ethics aside, we want to see what the artists and producers want to teach us about the influence of art, and also what they want to teach us through their art.

THE METHOD OF IMPACT

The documentary *Decadence: Decline of the Western World* explores the steady decline of the Judeo-Christian culture that has dominated the western world for over 300 years. The description of the film on IMDB declares: The West consumes without consequence, loves without longevity and lives without meaning[6]. The latter part of the film discusses media and religion. The narrator gives a prophetic summation about how our consumer lives are influenced by the media:

> We watch helplessly as our sons and daughters, mesmerized by pop-idols and Hollywood's cut-glass heroes, advertise for sex first and then maybe a relationship which soon enough reaches for the headache pill.

About two decades before Dunn wrote this prophetic statement, Alan Bloom wrote similar projections in the book, *The Closing of the American Mind*:

> Picture a thirteen-year-old boy sitting in the living room of his family home doing his math assignment while wearing his Walkman headphones or watching MTV. He enjoys the liberties

hard won over centuries by the alliance of philosophic genius and political heroism, consecrated by the blood of martyrs; he is provided with comfort and leisure by the most productive economy ever known to mankind; science has penetrated the secrets of nature in order to provide him with the marvelous, lifelike electronic sound and image reproduction he is enjoying. And in what does progress culminate? A pubescent child whose body throbs with orgasmic rhythms; whose feelings are made articulate in hymns to the joys of onanism or the killing of parents; whose ambition is to win fame and wealth in imitating the drag-queen who makes the music. In short, life is made into a nonstop, commercially prepackaged masturbational fantasy.[7]

How did we arrive at such a place where our freedoms lead us only to perversion? To examine how our culture slipped to this extreme is not an easy task and entire books have been written on the topic. I only hope to summarize some of the debate with the sheer intention of whetting your appetite to search for better personal conclusions on the matter. Examine everything carefully.

Musicians, film producers, video game programmers all agree their respective art affects us. But as George Lucas notes in the above quote, they do not want to admit they have any role in how bad the world is, but most want to declare that art makes the world a better place. It is true, from the Christian pop-artists to the thrash-metal bands, from the shamanistic styling of the Grateful Dead to the unique brand that is Frank Zappa, musicians, neurologists, and everyone else who looks casually at the facts will honestly agree: music greatly affects our disposition. Research is starting to mount that other forms of media entertainment also take hold on us, teaching us, forming us. Rand Salzman said it best: "Viewers simply cannot help but be 'rippled' by the emotional gut-wrenching influence of huge moving color images backed by stereo sound.[8]" The question remains is whether this emotional, gut-wrenching influence is a good influence or a bad influence on the consumers of such entertainment.

Some may argue the influence is negative. When school shootings and other violent acts are perpetrated by youth, some people are fast to point the finger at the violent songs, games, or movies often consumed by these kids. Such blaming is an oversimplification, however, on the other hand, many will suggest that their favorite music has no impact on their worldview; they merely 'like the beat'. That, too, is an oversimplification. The delivery as media is actually neutral, like money. The point of agreement among those with a positive view and those with a negative view is that music can affect the way we live, it can give us something to relate to, something by which to blow off steam, or something by which to teach us about our world.

During the initial influx of film into the American culture, it was very clear that the entertainment industry was going to change the way people lived their lives. During the 1920's, a series of morally questionable films, the murder of William Taylor, and a Hollywood rape prompted the proposal of several laws to place regulations on the film industry. Will Hays was appointed to produce a conduct guide for Hollywood film producers, a guide that became known as the *Hays Code*. The document begins by saying:

> If motion pictures consistently held up high types of character, presented stories that would affect lives for the better, they could become the greatest natural force for the improvement of mankind.[9]

The introduction to the document continues on to say entertainment and art are important influences in the life of a nation, thus the film entertainment is "directly responsible for spiritual or moral progress, for higher types of social life, and for much correct thinking." The code guided and directed the moral content of the film industry for over forty years, but some people whom did not agree with the code or the morality it proposed pushed the boundaries so far as to force the document into the ancient and out-dated relics of the American entertainment industry. The code was later replaced with the current rating system which will be discussed in more detail in chapter 8 of this book.

During these early years of film production and with consideration of the Hays Code, the realization that film does impact the moral disposition of its viewers, Warner Brothers adopted the slogan, "Good Citizenship with Good Picture Making". In the early years, the film company did focus on morally good films, but the steady decay

> The film industry merely produces what we pay to see.

began to erode the message and while to this day the company has an entire affiliated website dedicated to good citizenship, that may be exclusive lip service from the company that brought us such morally bankrupt films as *Natural Born Killers*. In all, despite the clear evidence film does morally direct the society, the film industry merely produces what we pay to see.

The power of film transcends beyond simple moral messages, and music can direct the listeners to the intended message the artist seeks to teach. With a full-on media campaign, anyone can convince even the most studious people to change their ways and adopt a belief system for which they generally do not believe. This was very clear by governments who started to use the power of film to change the minds and beliefs of its citizens into their own ideals. Although many people will point to the Russian (*Alexander Nevsky*) and German films (*Triumph of the Will*) that were used to turn the citizens of those countries into what amounted to war criminals in the reigns of Stalin and Hitler, the Italians and the United States were also among those using film for propaganda. Gerald Nye, a Republican senator from North Dakota, declared in a congressional meeting:

> When you go to the movies, you go there to be entertained...and then the picture starts-goes to work on you, all done by trained actors, full of drama, cunningly devised...Before you know where you are, you have actually listened to a speech designed to make you believe that Hitler is going to get you.

Nye was attempting to make the point that Hollywood was being transformed into a propaganda machine for war-mongering to change the American people's stance on World War II. Nye was against the Hollywood propaganda machine, but the President, Franklin D. Roosevelt, considered it necessary. In 1939 Nazi Germany was producing propaganda in a full-fledge media campaign to garner support for the Nazis under Joseph Goebbels. Roosevelt responded with using American film to sustain morale and according to Nancy Snow, Hollywood now acquired a prominent place in the battle for men's minds[10]. 1940 saw the creation of the Motion Picture Committee Cooperating for National Defense, the industry-wide organization that would produce military training films and patriotic films for the American people in order to gain support for a war effort that many Americans were not sure merited participation. The government only unofficially supported this effort, though after the entrance into World War II, FDR created a specific division in the government to inform Hollywood producers on ways to portray any manner of political matters from war and foreign policy to domestic affairs. Though it is unclear whether this direct influence is still enacted, officially, in 1949 an appropriations act restricted the use of public funds for "publicity and propaganda.[11]" Regardless of this act, film plays a large part in unifying the ideals in the people whom consume media.

Though we hear very little about it today, marketing itself is propaganda. Companies pay millions to place their products in movies, and in America today government-paid advertising on health care, political parties, food, defense, and social services can be observed daily on television and displayed as Internet advertising. Even the enemies of the United States use propaganda in order to garner support for their cause. Suicide bombers for Al Qaeda and likely also ISIS are recruited by viewing the successful explosions of other martyrs and hearing the praise for the perpetrator and seeing the community celebritizing the remaining family, showering them in riches. Such films and rallies gain support for the cause of suicide bombings and acquire willing people to carry out the acts[12]. Whether we are seeing a commercial for the latest laundry detergent or seeing a new spin on a political agenda, we are better off acting on our mind's sound logic rather than by the seductive, humorous, or emotionally appealing commercials.

Beyond propaganda, modern entertainment including movies, music, and video games desire to teach the consumers. The writers and producers want to convey a worldview or question the audience's presuppositions. This is not just a modern trend that cropped up in the last decade. As early as the 1920s, research was commenced to determine the influence movies exert over youth. The results of the studies determined teenagers learned how to dress, how to behave socially, and how to think about the world though film. Some movies, such as *The Crying Game* sought to question erotic love between same gender adults and *For a Lost Soldier* examined homosexuality in adult-child relationships. Both films were released in 1992, though the latter was a foreign film. These productions were very intentional in how they made the viewer question their presuppositions. Most movies have just as great an impact in a passive way like the manner in which dirty uncle Eddy can influence the kids into uncouth manners.

Taken together, these observations indicate media entertainment, in any form, can certainly convey a message to those who consume the art. The message is not entirely bad or entirely good. The creators and producers of the art cannot choose to positively impact the consumer because they wish to deny the negative consequences of bad media, but neither can someone decide a certain song or movie contains all negative impact based solely on the beat or the reputation of the band. All these taken together, we will consider next some special considerations surrounding music and video games and their role in impacting the consumers.

MUSIC AND SOUND

Music is all around us. While some want to dismiss music as a harmless pastime, most artists defend the positive impact of music in the world, though as Lucas admits, they do not want to admit the negative impacts. Even the MTV producers know about the impact that music can have on the listeners. One executive for the station said:

> Music tends to be a predictor of behavior and social values. You tell me the music people like and I'll tell you their views on abortion, whether we should increase our military arms, [and] what their sense of humor is like.[13]

Likewise, Michael Greene, the former president of the Grammy Music Awards, said in his 2000 speech:

> Music is a magical gift which we must nourish and cultivate in our children, especially now as scientific evidence proves that an education which includes the arts makes a better math and science student, enhances special intelligence in newborns, and let's not forget that the arts are a compelling solution to teen violence, they are certainly not the cause of it.[14]

Notice how Greene defends music as making students better at math and science, though those studies were conducted using classical music including Mozart and Beethoven, not the music the Grammy's generally support or award. He talks about music's impact in the newborn, and simply dismisses the clear impact it can have in rebellion of the listener. But his 2001 speech embraces the rebellion behind music:

> People are mad! And people are talking and that is a good thing, because it is through dialog and debate that social discovery and progress can occur. Listen, music has always been the voice of rebellion, it's a mirror of our culture, sometimes reflecting a dark and disturbing underbelly, obscured from the view of most people of privilege...We cannot edit out the art that is uncomfortable. Remember, that is what our parents tried to do to Elvis, the [Rolling] Stones, and the Beatles.[15]

Greene discusses a very true point, and it is one point that I am attempting to make in this book:

> Most of the adults who pass judgment have never listened to, or more to the point, have never even engaged their kids about the object of their contempt [the music]. This is not to say that there is not a lot of fear in this violence driven society of ours.[16]

I agree with Greene on this final point, but he does not go far enough. It is not a matter that we *just* need to look at the media our kids are consuming; we need to look at the media *we* are consuming because our kids model our own behavior before they will live out our instruction. We cannot blame music or movies entirely for the cultural decay Greene clearly admits, but we are foolish to think watching violent, sexual films or listening to violent, sexual music is just a meaningless distraction, since we already believe music alters our mental and emotional state. We must find a balance and consider that art does teach us and we will learn the messages they espouse whether we want to or not.

Michael Greene is not the only professional in the industry to believe music can cause tremendous positive impact while denying it's negative effect. To a degree, these people are correct. When the Columbine shooting occurred, Marilyn Manson was thrown under the bus as a major cause of the event, even though Klebold and Harris did not even like his music. Manson wrote an article in his own defense appearing in Rolling Stone magazine, and Manson does raise several great arguments. He writes:

> Responsible journalists have reported with less publicity that Harris and Klebold were not Marilyn Manson fans -- that they even disliked my music. Even if they were fans, that gives them no excuse, nor does it mean that music is to blame. Did we look for James Huberty's inspiration when he gunned down people at McDonald's? What did Timothy McVeigh like to watch? What about David Koresh, Jim Jones? Do you think entertainment inspired Kip Kinkel, or should we blame the fact that his father bought him the guns he used in the Springfield, Oregon, murders?[17]

Manson is not alone in the camp of artists who do not like to hear their art being blamed for violence in the culture. Some people echo the sentiment of a young heavy metal fan who said, "It's all fantasy, none of it is real, you can't take this seriously, it's just like a movie.[18]" Many artists over the years have been asked if they believe violence in music has any impact on the listeners, and their answer is generally a resounding 'No'. But that does not stop people from trying to blame music anyway. In a commentary blog, the author identified "Six Most Idiotic Attempts to Blame Musicians for Violent Events.[19]" The article was written on the heels of the attempted assassination of Gabrielle Giffords in Tucson. It appears the perpetrator was a big fan of the song, *Bodies Hit the Floor* which the artists, Deadpool, say the song is about the moshpits in heavy metal concerts (curious how we are in a relativistic world yet the violent interpretations are not accepted). Nevertheless, the connections have been made not only to this song, but others as well.

Some arguments suggesting that music plays a role in violence can seem valid, such as the teen suicide committed when a young man placed the Ozzy Osbourne song *Suicide Solution* on repeat while he hanged himself. The AC/DC song *Night Prowler* was blamed for the Richard Ramirez murders, and serendipitously, he accidentally left his AC/DC hat at one of the murder scenes! While researching about lessons learned from school shootings, the National Research Council and the Institute of Medicine researchers compiled a book depicting the warning signs and character traits of several high-profile shootings from the 1990's and it would appear violent music lyrics did have a role in the legal cases surrounding a copycat killing a month following Columbine[20]. These are just a few of the notable examples where music has been blamed in part for violent crimes.

Though I do not in any way suggest music is the root cause of violence and rebellion in our culture, I do not deny it may be a rather large contributing factor. I personally have listened to my fair share of horrible music including heavy metal and gangsta rap, but I for one have not gone out killing people. I do find it telling, however, that very few mass killers are not big fans of Beethoven although heavy and violent music more often than not is readily consumed by the young killers in our society.

Taken together, it is more likely music and movies reflect our nature back to us. As they become more violent, violence starts seeping out into the culture at large. So music may not cause the violence, but it is a reflection of the violence we feel inside ourselves, more of a mirror and less of a causation.

THE SOCIAL CONTROVERSY

C hristian organizations are not the only groups who tend to blame violent acts on violent music. A CNN article from London wrote that, "Heavy metal [music] is often used as a scapegoat to distract from the thoroughly more complicated societal problems surrounding [violence].[21]"

It is very true many cultural factors lend to violent behavior and criminal activity. Life is too complex for a single factor to be isolated as the sole determinant of violence in our society, and there are certainly studies that point to a calming effect of loud music among people who are already aggressive[22]. In the study, people who were angry listened to heavy music for a period of time before a being administered a measurement for anger. The result was a calming effect among the participants. But the study measured anger, not violent behavior, and those are not mutually exclusive to one another.

Further, I find it interesting the people who want to accept the great positive power of music while denying the ability for music to emotionally harm us tend to lay in the camp of creators and producers. The science, it would seem, paints a very different picture. One study published in the Journal of Personality and Social Psychology reported songs with violent lyrics can produce more aggressive emotions than similar songs without lyrical content[23]. The article is hardly the first of its kind. Similar studies have been conducted looking at whether the music alone causes more aggression than a music video, or if the lyrics that are difficult to decipher has any specific impact on the emotions of the listener. It turns out violent media of any kind will increase aggressive behavior in the consumer.

In his book on *Media Violence and Children*, Douglas Gentile discusses the specific impact and draw of violent music to teenagers and observes that though all young people have a degree of susceptibility to peer pressure, those teens that listened to heavy or violent music tended to be more influenced by their peers to engage in risky lifestyle choices. Gentile also cites one study that youth in juvenile detention were three times more likely to be fans of violent music than their peers. These same results applied to self-violent behavior including attempted suicide and self-inflicted wounds of other kinds[24].

These articles and reports are merely a tip of a very large iceberg of science examining the impact of music on our emotional state. In brief summary, music is not the sole, or may not even be the primary cause of violent behavior in the culture, but to omit it as harmless also may not be the correct response. Though many of the artists who produce the music in our culture accept that music can change us for the better, they never want to admit that it can change us for the worse. The scientists and social psychologists on the other hand hold a more balanced view, with experimentation, that some music styles and lyrics can give us great positive motivation but other styles will push us toward violence, discontent, and a negative world view.

DISTINGUISHING BEAT AND SOUND

Even though movies, television programs, and video games can evoke an emotional response in consumers, music stands out as the ultimate influence over our emotions. Most music, except the purely instrumental, can be divided into the impact of the musical rhythm and the impact of the lyrical content. Both should be considered when examining how and why music generates such an emotional response in the listeners. The most common argument in defense of listening to any music without thought is that the consumer 'likes the beat'. This can be a valid argument but it denies the power lyrics exert over our lifestyle. For many songs, we tap our toes to the rhythm and are sometimes oblivious to what the musician is actually saying to us. We also all know at least one song that is either instrumental or nearly so that really speaks to our heart; so part of this argument is certainly valid. The rhythm is important and can be a calming effect or an aggressor on our emotions. Louder music, however, does not always mean more aggressive. One study demonstrated that whatever music you heard around your house when you grew up tended to calm you down the most, so if you had the privilege of being raised by metal-heads, an Iron Maiden song may provide a relaxing emotional response in you. When I hear certain songs to this day, I am taken back to the events surrounding the circumstances when I first heard those songs, and it is the rhythm that takes me back, not the words. Knowing music can calm us or agitate us is a good starting point for understanding the message the artist intended to convey, whether through the words or through the beat.

Some musicians utilize shamanistic rhythms in an attempt to place their listeners into some sort of trance, though it is questionable they need to go to that extreme. Two artists who openly spoke of these music forms were Mickey Hart from The

Grateful Dead and John Densmore from The Doors. Even in Densmore's book, *Riders on the Storm*, he spoke of The Doors as wanting to produce music that made their audience reflect and come to a different conclusion about life[25]. While artists like Hart have intentionally traveled to shamanistic and eastern villages to learn about hypnotic music, other artists including Michael Jackson and Carlos Santana openly admit that 'some other force' directed their musical ability. Truly the rhythm affects both the musician and the audience.

Besides the rhythmic affect, the lyrical content in songs is also deeply consequential, and probably more directly so. Obviously the occasional hearing of a given song will not cause you to go kill someone or begin the practice of evoking demons. But how will we be changed over a period of time if we listen to a mental diet of hate, depression, death, and sex? Wayne Kramer echoed this exact sentiment while speaking about the mistakes his music group, MC5, made while they were young. He said:

> We endorsed the idea of violence...we didn't think that through well enough. In retrospect, once you use a language and the images of violence, you can't put the toothpaste back in the tube and you don't know where that is going to play out.[26]

Kramer went on to reference the violence in many gangsta rap groups and noted how many of those artists ended up getting shot. In my personal opinion as a former 2 Pac fan, much of his violent songs were more about the violence in that lifestyle and encouraged people to get out, not to get involved. But as we are ready consumers of media for the entertainment value rather than the message, we are more often negatively impacted by the content far before we would consider the warning proclaimed by artists. For this reason alone, we should always examine our entertainment choices very carefully.

Gaming Impact

S ince the early 2000's more focus has been aimed at video games as a possible contributing factor to violence in society. As games evolved over the years, they have become more complex, more realistic, and have pushed moral and social boundaries faster than other entertainment genres. Some games have even been banned in many countries, including the United States, because of the content they portrayed.

Video games started as merely passing amusement and entertainment. The first recorded video game was a version of pong, and then *Castles* was quickly introduced where you and an opponent took turns trying to shoot one another's castle taking into account the wind direction and the power of the cannon. Atari adapted the game in *Combat* where you could even move your tank around to shoot your opponent. Later on, a much improved version of this concept was born in the game *Worms* where each player controlled a team of worms armed to the hilt with grenades, guns, and other weapons of mass destruction. The object of course was to eliminate the other team.

All games have evolved over the years, usually building on the newer and better technologies. Eventually games reached such pristine graphical display that a colleague of mine, an avid gamer, placed a highway scene on his computer desktop that was so realistic, I did not even recognize it came from a video game. Of course, that game with such awesome graphics became one of the most violent video games yet on the market where shooting a target enough times would result in clearly identifiable organs to plop out of the dead body. Yes, the evolution of games was so complete that an old game of merely driving away from the police on a Frogger-like 8 bit display has led to the latest installment – clear-cut graphics including bloody violence, extensive vulgar and sexual scenes, and of course you move up the ranks by succeeding at the commission of violent crimes and drug deals. One game, *RapeLay*, banned in many countries, actually depicts the game hero roaming around stalking victims to rape. Depravity in video games knows no bounds and is only kept in check by slowly eroding laws intended to keep some games off of the public market.

The power of video games cannot be denied. Even though excellent times can be found with friends around modern video games, we should also consider that many games may contain scenes filthier than Hollywood productions. We must be as diligent to screen video games as we would movies and music. If music and television can positively or negatively change our hearts and minds, than video games can do that and more because we drive a part of the story with our intentional control of the character. Some have argued violence in video games lends itself to muscle memory and news articles have noted some shootings have occurred before the shooter was cognizant of the attack, though the small number of reports indicate this is more of the exception than the rule.

> We must be as diligent to screen video games as we would movies and music.

Aside from the mental impact the games exert over our thoughts, we must also consider their time consumption. Modern games have a very high propensity to be addictive and for the ten or so percent of the population struggling with an addictive personality, certain video games may be like a bottle of vodka is to a drunk. Before we realize it, we can find ourselves totally sucked into the digital world. Though more could be said of this topic, chapter 7 covers addiction in detail including the types of games with the highest addictive potential. For now, know that video games are a double edged sword which handled improperly, can lead to chronic time-wasting and moral, spiritual, or mental decay.

Though the anecdotal evidence has been communicated by the news, parents, and others, actual science surrounding video games has been conducted since such amusements were first available on the market. In a 2009 literature review by social researchers at Iowa State University, the effects of video games, both positive and negative, were documented[27]. This summary report documents research depicting the positive outcomes of video game playing including improved hand-eye coordination, increased response to field of vision testing, increased performance on special arrangement tests, and much positive movement in online education. Absent from this article is the positive use of modern movement-sensory games that have increased American exercise in a culture where video games seem to be more important than staying healthy. Based on these reports, we are foolish to bar video games entirely from our lives.

However, the science does not merely paint a positive picture of video game involvement. As many people have surmised, several negative outcomes were also observed in video game consumers. First, is a prominent physiological response resembling the activation of the so-called 'fight or flight' response. Though this can be a useful state in specific circumstances, the researchers point out that this effect is also present in violent and aggressive behavior. In fact, playing violent video games (the kinds most often studied) generally increases all parameters of psychological aggression testing including feelings, cognition, and behavior. Unfortunately, most of the studies conducted on the topic of video game impact have been short-term studies, however one report following grade-school children who played violent video games over a two year period indicated regular consumption of such games increased their long-term aggression in school. The research on video games is still new and better experiments are already being conducted. Suffice it to say for now that some video games may not merely be just *passive* entertainment.

UNIFYING THE MEDIA-CENTRIC CULTURE

In the first chapter I eluded to media entertainment becoming more aligned and unified. We are living in times where we are connected 24/7 to the whole world at all times except when we sleep. Between our phones, computers, tablets, and television sets, the typical American is always online, viewing advertising, and tempted to put down work to be entertained. The industry has been collecting our data for long enough to know how to hook us to extract our hard-earned dollars. In the recent months, more and more companies and products are teaming up to sell us two products in one commercial, though I have seen it most recently with a movie and a product. I noted in the first chapter that the star of the show and other popular actors are selling more and more products. Now it is not just the actors, but the star of the program such as Captain America selling Audi or Star Wars heroes selling…well, EVERYTHING! The media is unifying against us to sell their products and messages.

Media is becoming more unified every day. The entertainment industry has combined our favorite stars, our favorite movies, our favorite bands together with one another in order to form a unified front with a sole purpose. They would like us, at all times, to be buying what they are selling. Megadeth wrote, *Peace Sells, but Who's Buyin'* about military tactics and cold-war policies. We could easily say, Ads Sell, but Who's Buyin' to counter this spread. We watch television and before we know it Captain America is selling us a Audi, and I can't get a box of macaroni and cheese without some cartoon character plastered on the box and with noodles in the shape of the character. We are hooked on media, listening to their messages, buying their products, and often to the detriment of our body as we lack exercise, our mind as we are constantly inputting their messages, and our spirit as the power of God within us atrophies like seeds choked out by the weeds that is our media entertainment. In the next chapter, we will examine the messages these artists and producers are teaching us, but in the mean time, perhaps Marilyn Manson was right:

> In my work I examine the America we live in, and I've always tried to show people that the devil we blame our atrocities on is really just each one of us. So don't expect the end of the world to come one day out of the blue – it's been happening every day for a long time.[28]

CHAPTER QUESTIONS

1. How have you considered the meaning behind media entertainment in the past? How has your view changed?

2. Have you had ethics classes? On what basis were those ethics presented?

3. What type of media impacts you the most?

4. In what ways does media direct our thinking?

5. What are your favorite bands? What messages do their lyrics teach?

6. What video games do you play? Is there a story line? What does it teach?

3

THE MEANING BEHIND THE MESSAGE

The unexamined life is not worth living
– Socrates

December 14th, 2012 was one of the coldest days in American history. A young man wandered into an elementary school to commit one of the worse murder scenes our country has ever seen. In a span of only five minutes the shooter killed 26 elementary-aged children before turning the gun on himself. The song *Pumped Up Kicks* by Foster the People was popular on the radio at the time[29]:

> All the other kids with the pumped up kicks
> You better run, better run, outrun my gun
> All the other kids with the pumped up kicks
> You better run, better run, faster than my bullet

Within a week the song was pulled from broadcast in the top radio station in Los Angeles, the home of Hollywood preaching 'the arts only change us for the better'. Subsequently, many other radio stations followed suit, dropping the song from their playlist[30]. If music is just about the beat, than what is the point of taking a wildly popular song off air? Despite the normal banter about music "just being harmless songs," this removal of popular music from radio air-time is not an isolated incident. After the shooting at Columbine high school in 1999, Marilyn Manson became the poster-child of 'evil' and was blamed in part for the massacre at the hands of Harris and Klebold. Manson canceled several concerts on his present tour out of respect for the families. Though Manson initially declined most interviews, he finally spoke to several news outlets when it became apparent he needed to fashion a response[31,32].

Music is not the ultimate source of violence in our culture, but it cannot be denied as a contributing factor toward our general societal coarsening typically culminating in violence and immorality. Media entertainment as a means of delivery is completely neutral. A film or a song can inspire deep positive motivation or loathsome hatred in the consumer. A film or documentary can give us information by which to challenge our life presuppositions, and such change could better direct the course of our lives. In short, media entertainment is like money: it is neither good nor bad. The course of impact on its recipients is directly related to the message it contains. We can use ten thousand dollars to buy food for a dozen families, pay their bills in their need, and relieve some stress in their life so they can become stabilized. But, I can waste that same sum of money in Las Vegas on riotous living spending it just as fast, but in ways failing to bring honor or glory to anyone. Money spent on gambling, prostitutes, alcohol, drugs, and the like would be a poor use of money, but helping others in needful times will result in a blessing to those that give and those that receive. So it is with media entertainment: **The medium is neutral, the message is consequential**.

Media entertainment, whether music, movies, video games, or any other means of delivery, teaches us life lessons indiscriminate of our desire to learn. Because we have no choice in the matter, it is wisest if we know what 'course' we are taking through our entertainment. We should seek to know the artists, the messages, the intentions, and the motivations behind the art we are consuming. Just because music is Christian does not mean that it is theologically sound, or even right to hear at all times, and just because music is secular that does not mean the music is worthless. David did say, "*I will set nothing worthless before my eyes (Psalm 101:3)*". He did not say, "I will set nothing non-Christian before my eyes." It is not a matter of just Christian or non-Christian, we need to be deeper thinkers than that if we want to navigate our Christian lives in an impactful way before the world.

The artists and producers in our modern culture are generally teaching us out of their personal world-views. Harvey Fierstein produced the *Torch Song Trilogy* as a play and later an HBO special to teach that homosexuality is just an alternative lifestyle. He said in interviews about his various productions that they were to teach as well as entertain. His desire for us was to adopt a view of life where homosexuality was commonplace, this was in the 1980's and 1990's when the homosexual conversation was still taboo, even on MTV. Two decades later, as I write this chapter the supreme court has just ruled in favor of constitutionally protecting homosexual marriage, legalizing the unions in all American states. As you can see, one bold man stepping out to produce a taboo film may have been a contributing factor to the broad-scale legalization of homosexual marriage. Do not think, however, that the impact only affects the liberal agenda. Though days of Hollywood's past brought us righteous films including *Sergeant York*, *Ben Hur*, and *The Ten Commandments*, but even those were before my time. I cannot recall one movie from my childhood depicting a true version of Christianity where the central characters demonstrated real faith, love, and the redemptive power of God. During a dark period in Hollywood when Christian movies were taboo, Mel Gibson produced *The Passion of the Christ* boldly against his detractors.

Since the movie debuted, many Godly Christian films have penetrated the market.

In many cases, the message is secondary to the profits, but the consumer attachment to the media is based in part on the represented artist. A favorite star actor can drive just as many ticket sales as a marketing campaign, and we all know that before anyone hears a new music album, the fans will rush to purchase music from their idols as soon as the tunes are released. The emotional appeal of the artists drives the sales, and the network provides the platform for the artist to perform. Robert Pittman, the founder of MTV said, "The strongest appeal is emotional. Here at MTV, we do not shoot for the fourteen year olds...we own them.[33]" MTV had a desire from the beginning to push and promote a separate youth culture as a means to recapture the dwindling music entertainment business. The producers of the network performed more market research than any other endeavor at the time resulting in many markets reporting teenage audience consumers greater than 40-80% saturation after only a few years, particularly interesting because at the time, cable television was still not very popular in America. Their absolute target was the teenage audience, and they made their money by inserting themselves between the youth and their parents, applying pressure, and giving artists a platform to produce a counter culture[34]. If the messages they want to teach are messages driving positive impact on culture, that is great, but often the message is one of evil and rebellion, thus we have reason to be concerned about ourselves and our children who consume modern entertainment. As we embark here in looking at the messages of a few popular artists, I will use verified sources taking the

> MTV made their money by inserting themselves between the youth and their parents producing a counter culture

comments and lessons from the mouth of the artists themselves. Let's see the types of things that they want to teach us.

SELF-PROCLAIMED ANTI-CHRIST

S ome artists may very well be merely entertaining, but of all of the musicians I have known over the years, and all of those whom I have read about have felt very passionately about their art, and they usually do desire to tell people the meaning behind their songs. For other artists, the teaching is the reason they are producing their music. Brian Warner, better known as Marilyn Manson is one such artist who makes no effort to hide his simple message: he wants to destroy Christianity and the values that it claims to stand for:

> At the time, I was reading books about philosophy, hypnosis, criminal psychology and mass psychology. On top of that, I was completely bored, sitting around watching *Wonder Years* reruns and talk shows and realizing how stupid Americans were. All of this inspired me to create my own science project and see if a white band that wasn't rap could get away with acts far more offensive and illicit than 2 Live Crew's dirty rhymes. As a performer, I wanted to be the loudest, most persistent alarm clock I could be, because there didn't seem like any other way to snap society out of its Christianity- and media-induced coma.[35]

Manson is openly not just anti-Christian, he promotes himself as a Satanist. A classmate of his wrote: "Brian Warner and I were in the same class at Christian School in Canton, Ohio. Both Brian and I rejected the religious pressure of our education quite strongly. He, of course, promotes himself as a Satanist." His scorn for religion came from a very hypocritical upbringing in the church and in religious private school. Since that time he has viewed Christianity as merely fake. As a result, Manson has dedicated his life to toppling Christianity and his message is clear. He writes about his first meeting with Anton Szandor LaVey, the founder of the Church of Satan in San Francisco, that, "we had both dedicated the better part of our lives to toppling Christianity with the weight of its own hypocrisy, and as a result been used as scapegoats to justify Christianity's existence.[36]"

Manson is a shock rocker, but I am not entirely convinced that his antics are exclusively for show, but rather, they may be an extension of his life. His controversy can draw free media attention; convenient since he created his own persona of a person who is easy to hate. The opening dedication to his autobiography, *A Long Hard Road Out Of Hell* declares, "To Barb and Hugh Warner, May God forgive them for bringing me into this world." To create his persona (originally to write anonymously for a periodical), he wanted a name to highlight his belief that everyone has elements both of good and evil within themselves. The Marilyn part was most noted for glamour, but the actress of her namesake possessed a little darkness in sex appeal. Likewise Manson was one of the most evil people of his day yet had a small element of good mostly expressed in charisma. The name Marilyn Manson was chosen to highlight the good and evil present in all of us. The name stayed with Manson as a brand to spread his message. Manson wrote about the persona, "He was a character who, because of his contempt for the world around him and, more so, himself, does everything he can to trick people into liking him. And then, once he wins their confidence, he uses it to destroy them.[37]"

About his music, Manson describes also how one of his songs is about a popular televangelist saying how bad the world is and then asking for credit card donations while on another channel in the hotel room at the same time had a less-than-couth presentation also asking for a credit card. He wrote that his song

Cake and Sodomy was "An anthem for a hypocritical America slobbering on the tit of Christianity, it was a blueprint for our future messages. If televangelists were going to make the world seem so wicked, I was going to give them something real to cry about.[38]"

Manson is very clear about his life, his purpose, and his music. To him, it is all about pushing people away from Christianity. If he could destroy the faith, he would as simple as that. Music gives the world some evil and controversy to talk about, and he does what he can to destroy faith in the lives of his listeners. He is very clear about the purpose of his life and his music, and one need only to investigate that message from his own writing to discern what he boldly declares. Despite his attempts, however, Josh McDowell declared Christianity is a bell that has worn out many an anvil, and Manson will find that his message will grow silent to the praises delivered to Jesus Christ.

CHANT AND BE HAPPY

George Harrision of The Beatles (and by his influence The Beatles themselves) became infatuated with the Hare Krishna movement. The book *Chant and Be Happy* was written to garner support of the Hare Krisna faith by compiling interviews with George Harrison and John Lennon among others in order to support the spiritual causes of the early 1980's. The author, A.C. Bhaktivedanta Swami Prabhupada was praised as the spiritual master "who brought the transcendental teachings of Lord Krsna, including the authorized science of reincarnation, to the Western World." The book opens with a statement by George Harrison:

Everybody is looking for KRSNA. Some don't realize that they are, but they are. KRSNA is GOD, the Source of all that exists, the Cause of all that is, was, or ever will be. As GOD is unlimited, HE has many Names. Allah-Buddha-Jehova-Rama: All are KRSNA, all are ONE. By serving GOD through each thought, word, and DEED, and by chanting of HIS Holy Names, the devotee quickly develops God-consciousness. By chanting Hare Krsna, Hare Krisna Krisna Krisna, Hare Hare Hare Rama, Hare Rama Rama Rama, Hare Hare; one inevitably arrives at KRSNA Consciousness.[39]

We probably do not need to continue on in discussing Harrison's view of God, but since the Beatles and Harrison, were so popular that even among church-going adults and youth today they are hailed as gods themselves, let us continue to examine his statements lest we take anything out of context.

In the preface of the book, the author writes about how we achieve "unlimited and imperishable happiness." We only need to chant a simple sixteen word mantra the great teachers of India have called the Great Chant for Deliverance. The first chapter of the book is a 1982 interview with George Harrison. In the 2012 ebook updated edition, the editors note that "George Harrison was the impetus for the Beatles' spiritual quest of the sixties, and up until his death in 2001, the chanting of the Hare Krsna ... continued to play a key role in his life.[40]" Harrison's role in the Hare Krsna faith was not just a passing interest. He actually co-signed on the lease for the first Krsna temple in central London and bought Bhaktivedanta Manor for the religious leaders to teach the people about Krsna consciousness. He also financed the first printing of the book, Krsna.

Mukunda, Harrison's interviewer confirmed that George was "a member of the Beatles, undoubtedly the greatest single pop group in music history – one that influenced not only music but a whole generation of young people." Harrison responded that while he was still young he had seen it all, had it all, and looked onto what was next and determined there is more to life than money and fame. A spiritual journey was his next step, but Harrison's view of spirituality has to do with chanting, either the Hare Krsna or japa yoga, a specific format of chanting on beads. He described the importance of constantly chanting by saying, "The word Hare is the word that calls upon the energy that's all around the Lord. If you say the mantra enough, you build up an identification with God...and by chanting His names we connect with Him." It is clear George believes chanting is the way to know God, even saying such chanting makes a person pure.

While speaking on experiencing God through the senses, he says "to experience God through all the senses – not just by experiencing Him on Sunday, through your knees by kneeling on some hard wooden kneeler in the church. But if you visit a temple, you can see pictures of God, you can see the Deity form of the Lord." Later Harrison describes the full experience includes "chanting, dancing, philosophy, and prasada [vegetarian food that has been spiritualized by being offered to Lord Krsna].[41]"

George did not merely practice the art of Hare Krsna, he used his influence as a musician to spread the faith both overtly and subversively. He recorded a single called *The Hare Krsna Mantra* that became a hit single in many countries. Speaking of that record he said, "it's all a part of service...in order to try to spread the mantra all over the world. Also, to try and give the devotees a wider base and a bigger foothold in England and everywhere else.[42]" He says directly his purpose was to infiltrate society by producing a copy of the mantra that was short enough to play on the radio. In another song, *Awaiting On You All*, Harrison directly spoke of Krsna theology by suggesting merely chanting the names of God can free us from the material world. The album *All Things Must Pass* was a virtual hidden advertisement for the Krsna movement which led many people to the faith. The song *Living in the Material World* is a song influenced by Srila Prabhupada whom taught George about the Krsna life. The song ends, "Got to get out of this place by the Lord Sri Krsna's grace, my salvation from the material world." His song *That Which I Have Lost* was directly from the Bhagavad-gita (Hindu scriptures). And if these songs were not enough, Mukunda has an entire discussion on the most subversive song on the list: *My Sweet Lord.* Mukunda says, "I don't think it's possible to calculate just how many people were turned onto Krsna consciousness by your song '*My Sweet Lord.*'" Quoting from Harrison's auto-biography, Mukunda describes some of the soul-searching that occurred before the production of the song. George writes, "I wanted to show Hallelujah and Hare Krsna are quite the same thing. I did the voices singing 'Hallelujah' and then the change to 'Hare Krsna' so that people would be chanting the maha-mantra – before they knew what was going on![43]" In the interview after hearing the quote from his book, Harrison adds to his statements saying Hallelujah is a joyous expression for Christians, but Hare Krsna has a mystical side that puts us closer to God than Christianity represents Him. He continues,

> My idea in '*My Sweet Lord,*' because it was a pop song, was to sneak up on them a bit. The point was to have the people not offended by Hallelujah, and by the time it gets to Hare Krsna they're already hooked and their feet are tapping, and they're already singing Hallelujah – to kind of lull them into a sense of security. And then suddenly it turns into Hare Krsna, and they will all be singing that before they know what's happened, and they will think, 'Hey, I thought I wasn't supposed to like Hare Krsna?[44]'

We can see Harrison was very overt about his beliefs and used his music to spread his Krsna faith throughout the world. It may even be true that if the Beatles were not as successful as they were or the Krsna faith never crossed paths with Harrison, the whole movement may have died many years ago, at least where the west is concerned. Though the movement did help many people living on the streets in San Francisco and New York (mostly the hippies during their moment), the practicality of the religion leaves much to be desired.

CRAZY CLOWNS AND THE FBI

Another group whom is vocal about their beliefs is the Insane Clown Posse. Though this group is not as well known, they have provided significant contributions to hip-hop music, they have created the most solidified fan-base of any rock group, and have won more platinum records than any other independent artists. They are also vocal about the message behind their music. Violent J, one of the groups two front-men said in an article in The Vice, "Usually the message [of our music] is second to the entertainment and it's a hidden message.[45]" Their music has been routinely cited by critics as boring and simple, but their messages ring through in their strangely audible lyrics (at least audible relative to other music in the genre). The band admits their lyrical message is unified in many respects. They routinely call their fans by the organized name, The Juggalos, and their first several albums came together in one central theme finally revealed as specifically a religious communication. This is not a matter of subjective debate at least where the musicians themselves are concerned.

The Insane Clown Posse released their first album, *Carnival of Carnage*, as a direct interpretation of the inner city Detroit gang violence scene. A scene they have personally contributed to in their youth. The album contains dark themes about taking the violence in these inner city neighborhoods and setting it in

67

suburbia where such violence is generally not present. This recording launched a series of albums called the *Joker Card Deck* which contains six theme albums centering around their religion of *The Dark Carnival*. Each card, or album, is a theme about some aspect of this 'faith', which many fans did not even realize at the time of the release. Violent J breaks down all of the intended meanings in an interview with The Rolling Stone[46]. Their religion breaks down as follows: The *Carnival of Carnage* as we said is about taking the violence of the inner city to suburbia. The *Ringmaster* album confronts the listener with the final 'beast' they must wrestle upon leaving this world. The more you sin in this world, the bigger your beast. If you win, I guess things go well, the album does not clarify. The *Riddle Box* is about the age-old question: what would happen to you if you died right now. If you 'turn the crank', what comes out of the box. If you have lived a sinful life, the devil will pop out of the box, but if you have lived a righteous life, God will meet you when you turn the crank. *The Great Milenko* is a theme centered around the fantasies of people. The tempting voice, or the devil on your shoulder as it were. This is the great illusionist who convinces you that doing bad things will make your life fulfilled. If you fall to his temptations, "then you end up doing the [stuff], and you end up in jail and going to hell and all that.[47]" *The Amazing Jeckel Brothers* is an album about balancing sins. The two brothers are the positive side (Jake) and your negative side (Jack). Violent J says, "They're juggling these fireballs that are actually your evil deeds, your sins." If they manage to juggle your sins, then you are accepted into heaven. Then comes the final judgment. The band concluded this series with two more albums both with a common theme: The afterlife. Two wraith albums: *Shangri-La* was the album about the afterlife in heaven and *Hell's Pit* was about the afterlife in hell. The Dark Carnival was complete, and the band broadcast its message to the world[48]:

When we speak of Shangri-La, what you think we mean?
Truth is we follow God, we've always been behind him
The carnival is God, and may all Juggalos find him!

The Insane Clown Posse wanted to bring a deeper message to their fan-base[49]. The messages they proclaimed were ones rife with 'moral' messages about being good and finding God, and a warning not to let your sin outweigh your good deeds. Though their central message is one of morality, they are also outspoken and controversial, inciting rebellion (such to the extent they could barely find venues to perform), and rapping about horribly violent and obscene anger fantasies. The general themes in their violent music contain some trademarks. The first is usually the clown makeup. The group themselves will not perform, meet with media, or have any public appearances without their trademark white and black makeup; a theme also present in their many 'first person' style songs including *To Catch a Predator*[50]:

The house is getting funky, bodies in the basement stinking
What the [@#$%] am I thinking?
I put my face paint on, go downstairs and
beat they [butt] sometimes cuz it ease my mind

Another theme is violence, specifically wielding a hatchet[51]:

I rode into town with my axe in my holster
Everybody knows about the wicked piggy roaster
The sheriff at the border, he tried to take me out
I drew my axe with the quickness and cut his Adams apple out!

Another theme is the target of their violent lyrics. They are not just targeting anyone like the protagonists in *Natural Born Killers;* they are generally targeting people whom they perceive to be perpetrators, which is far more dangerous. The problem is the definition of perpetrator is subjective in many cases, and Insane Clown Posse does not mask the target of their violence. Referencing the two songs above, *To Catch a Predator* is objectively about violence against child molesters. The lyrics of the song depict Violent J posing as a teenage girl online to lure in a predator to torture and kill. Violent J told a journalist, "In our music, we express a lot of anger. A lot of anger we express is still very real. It's just easier to say it on your record, and it's amplified on our records. If we talk about killing a pedophile, that comes from somewhere. That's real anger. We wish we could kill a pedophile, so we do it on the albums.[52]" I also believe that pedophilia is a bad thing, but killing without due process is simply called murder, and these messages seem to promote such acts. To contrast this song, *Piggy Pie* (old school version) is specifically about targeting three types of people. Though some people have said the first piggy is also about pedophilia, the lyrics seem to suggest more incestuous acts than anything else:

He likes to [have sex with] his sister and drink his moonshine
A typical redneck, filthy...swine

The second piggy is more objective. The band begins to rap about the slaughter of police officers:

He lays down his rules and reads you your rights
In that funny looking car with the little blinking lights

...

To the piggy station and lay on the horn
First piggy out- we blow his lungs out his uniform

The third piggy in their song is wealthy people, those who they perceive "this little piggy must definitely die". This song introduces hatred for people with more financial success than themselves, hatred for law and order in our society, and a strong message of violence. We have already discussed music itself does not specifically cause people to go out and commit violent crimes, however, the tightness of the fan-base combined with the commonality of similar violent crimes surrounding the Insane Clown Posse concerts finally led the FBI to place the Juggalos on a gang list for 'loosely organized gangs'. In a lawsuit, the band sought to fight the FBI for their evidence of the classification, but the bureau responded with the original list citing violence in several cities linked to their concerts. In all, the Insane Clown Posse is very vocal about finding God and doing good deeds, but it would appear that most of their good deeds include killing people who are successful, killing police, and becoming subjective vigilantes wiping out anyone with whom they do not agree. Such 'morality' is nothing more than self-righteousness.

We have seen from three separate artists they did not merely produce music, but produced an agenda with which to teach their listeners. In Marilyn Manson's case he wants to topple Christian values because of what he perceives as being mere hypocrisy. In the case of George Harrison, his intent is to spread eastern religions that teach all gods are the same, so you should existentially choose your own path. The Insane Clown Posse is interested in a works-based subjective religion where your good deeds and sins are on a scale and your final destiny is controlled by your actions, but their faith is subjectively based on what they feel is right. Clearly these musicians are trying to teach us things that are not amusing to God.

THE RESULT OF THE LIFESTYLE

The lifestyle of many of the popular musicians is the ultimate testament to the messages they preach and the lifestyles guiding them. Very few popular stars live lives infused with even basic integrity, though I do not intend to say they are all going straight to hell. Our chapter is not one of judgment or condemnation, but one of examination. We are not telling them how to live their lives, but we need to consider the influences guiding ourselves daily. Our questions should be simple: What are the beliefs and guiding principles of the stars? Do I want to emulate the lifestyle of the famous? Can the stars guide us in ways that are moral and God-honoring? When we know the answers to these questions, we should be able to grasp the importance of examining the lifestyles usually accompanying stardom.

The alleged 27 club refers to the number of artists, usually musicians, who have died around the age of 27. We will not consider the conspiracy theories surrounding those deaths, but at the same time, we will also be considering the stars whom have left the planet much earlier than our modern longevity statistics would have predicted. The early deaths of these artists is tragic, and their existence

> Their existence would be in vain if we did not seek to learn something from their life and honor them in their death.

would be in vain if we did not seek to learn something from their life and honor them in their death. Not all of these deaths were related to the lifestyles the artists lived such as the loss of Buddy Holly and Lynyrd Skynyrd to plane crashes. Even Lars Allrich from Metallica was claimed by an accident that had nothing to do with drinking or drugs, however the percentage of deaths due to 'lifestyle misadventure' of one form or another is shocking. Yes, at least two stars, Bon Scott of AC/DC and Brian Jones of Rolling Stone actually list Lifestyle Misadventure on their death certificate. Young was found dead as a result of alcohol toxicity in his automobile. Perhaps if more coroners actually listed drugs and alcohol as the cause of death of these superstars rather than benign phrases like 'asphyxiation' more young people in particular might exclude drugged-out rockstars from their personal circle of influence.

Drug abuse is the one killer that has ultimately claimed many famous lives. Jimi Hendrix, Jim Morrison, Janis Joplin, Elvis Presley, to name a few, died of complications from consuming illegal drugs. Movie actors are not immune to these negative effects. Such talented young actors as River Pheonix and Brad Renfow left the earth way too early due to their active drug abuse. Alcohol takes many more stars and fans of stars through either drunk driving accidents or some degree of alcohol toxicity. Violence claims some, particularly in the world of rap. 2Pac and many other rappers are fired upon in the turmoil of the gang culture that many warn their audience against. Coolio wrote in the famous song *Gangsta's Paradise*[53]:

> You better watch how you're talking and where you're walking
> Or you and your homies might be lined in chalk
> I really hate to trip but I gotta loc
> As they croak, I see myself in the pistol smoke, fool
> I'm the kinda G the little homies wanna be like
> On my knees in the night saying prayers in the streetlight

Many artists have grown up in the violent culture including the popular hiphop scene that has arisen in gang-ridden Detroit. Eminem, Kid Rock, and Insane Clown Posse are just a few of the famous rappers from that neglected and violent inner-city. They were the lucky ones who lived, but many more in that scene have not. Still some artists see the 'Suicide Solution' as their way out, and let's not forget those whom have contracted sexually transmitted diseases during the course of their career. The band Queen was cut short by Freddie Mercury dying of AIDS at the age of 45, a result of his homosexual lifestyle. Too many artists have had much left to give the world when their lifestyle caught up with them and took them away.

The artists who died are only some of the examples who could teach us valuable lessons. Those that have survived the early years of their career in the limelight tell many tales in the books about their lives, mistakes, and exploits. Their books tell of the great times they have had, but the fun can frequently be over-shadowed by painful addictions, regrettable life choices, and a wake of shattered relationships. Alice Cooper was such an alcoholic that he could not sleep unless a beer was placed on the nightstand awaiting him in the morning. He tells that he was so sick he had to be medically treated to withdraw from the alcohol prior to committing himself to rehab[54]. Likewise, Ozzy Osbourne described attending Alcoholic Anonymous meetings daily to battle the drugs and alcohol that plagued his life and career[55]. The wounded warrior is crippled by the demons in the bottle, but with the sobering reality that their livelihood, identity, and purpose was so tied up in life that they could barely function, and to break the addiction would be to radically change their way of providing an income. Alice Cooper described that he needed to put on the caricature of Alice to perform his concerts, but that he needed alcohol to put on that person. Talk about being stuck between the expectations of fans and the addictive bottle.

Nikki Sixx was an idol of my own childhood since I grew up listening to Mötley Crüe. The outspoken purpose of their band was to push the glam and the party scene, and Nikki took it several steps too far even according to the rest of his band mates. Sixx wrote down his story in an autobiographical release of his journals during the *Girls, Girls, Girls* tour the Crüe played in the late 1980's. He describes that his horrible addictions should serve as a warning to the younger generations as he describes actually dying twice in that period of time, once even being left for dead in a dumpster in London. Alice Cooper, who knew both Sixx and Jim Morrison said that Nikki reminded him of Morrison but was surprised that Nikki actually survived the tour describing his drug abuse as being more extreme than even Jim. His journal begins on Christmas day in 1986 as he describes himself as, "Naked under the Christmas tree with a needle in my arm and clutching a shotgun". Now his reformed purpose is to help save people from his own former lifestyle. He hopes his writings will perhaps prevent at least one young fan from following in his former footsteps[56].

The few examples herein are merely a sampling of the volumes we could explore on this topic. At any given moment we can check the news and see the sheer number of actors and musicians being arrested for DUI, overdosing on drugs, or exchanging life partners. Many stars have said the fame pushed them to the drugs as a result of dealing with the loneliness after leaving the stage. Others, like Nikki Sixx, have said the stardom merely provided the excess money needed to buy the extravagant amount of drugs. Other actors and musicians needed to numb the feelings of being pulled into the industry and shuttled around at the whim of the producers so that all of the monetary value could be extracted from the performer. The addictions plaguing the limelight are ever before our eyes, and between the lifestyle lessons famous artists teach us and the morally bankrupt way they live their lives, it is surprising how much we look to these people for our amusement since the entertainment informs our worldview.

Escaping Through Hell's Closing Gates

Not all actors and musicians die in their prime, nor do all continue to be drug and alcohol abusers through their whole life. Some artists end up hitting bottom at some point in their career resulting in lifestyle adjustments. Alice Cooper was a total slave to his addictions and has become outspoken about his sobriety in recent years. Eminem, Nikki Sixx, Marilyn Manson, Ozzy Osbourne, and Brian Head to name just a few found themselves knocking on death's door to find that no one was home. Whether from their own overdoses, or like Anthony Kiedis, the overdose of a close friend, many stars have cleaned up their act and and became vocal in their fight against the drugs once firmly rooted in their life.

Eminem grew up always moving causing him to lack stability in his home life. The tensions and opportunities led him to take pills of various forms leading to an overdose that left him about two hours from death. As a result of his abuse, he took a five year break from writing and performing, even reporting that he had to learn to rap again after near fatal organ failure. He came back strong, with energy, and with a new song *Not Afraid* about his drug habits and offering a helping hand others battling drug addiction. He wrote[57]:

> I'm not afraid
> To take a stand
> Everybody
> Come take my hand
> We'll walk together, through the storm
> Whatever weather, cold or warm
> Just letting you know that you're not alone
> Holler if you feel you've been down the same road

He is concerned not only with himself, but with telling his story about addiction. Like others before him who came out of dependence, he has a desire to never go back, and also to help others out.

Nikki Sixx writes of his multiple encounters with death within a single year. After a near-death experience sent him to the hospital he woke up and decided it was time to get sober. That marked the initial bout with sobriety. He wrote the album *Dr. Feelgood* while being entirely sober, the first in his career. The high reception and quality of the album was attributed to the band's desire to get clean. Though Sixx struggled with drugs on several single occasions since his initial wakeup call, he finally declared victory over substance abuse even during the turmoil of his second divorce. His book, *The Heroine Diaries*, is his project created with the hopes it will help his fans get off and stay off drugs. The proceeds of his book are donated to the same facilities that helped him discover sobriety.

Ozzy Osborne, the 'Prince of Darkness' is another story of sobriety worth the read. He describes how Black Sabbath started as just a band with influences in blues and rock, but how it was the marketers who created the persona of evil. Their first album was recorded in a single day en route to a concert and when they came back, the album proofs were ready. It was not their idea to include the pentagrams, evil personas, and other marks of the new breed of heavy metal emerging from England. The controversy, however, fueled the success of the band, and they never put an end to it, considering it just a made up facet of their lives; no one in the band took it seriously. However, it did catch the eye of the public, some decrying the band of leading youth toward evil, others thinking this new appearance was just cool. As for the band itself, the success merely fueled what they liked to do: party. And once the party started, it would not stop for several years. Ozzy himself fell to his success as the record label sent him drugs, booze, and girls on every tour. He became completely addicted, and he could not give up his music because it fueled his habits, and he could not give up his habits, because they were fueled by his success. He was trapped, forced into the character we have seen, and I think it is more indicative of the forces behind the industry more than the industry itself. Ozzy eventually had a somewhat happy story having cleaned himself up from drugs, but he was left scarred for life, the victim of his own success[58].

Some artists do not just escape the drug and alcohol abuse. They escape the 'kingdom of the ruler of the air *(Ephesians 2:2)'*. The first biography of a rock star I read was recommended from a student in our campus ministry. Brian Head, the former front man for the band Korn wrote about his life on the road and how the addictions overcame him, taking over his life. Waking up many times curious as to the happenings of the previous evening, he began to struggle with the deeper meaning of life. His book is called *Save Me From Myself* and it details the drugs and parties common not just with Korn, but with many of the tour scenes. He finally left the band to pursue a life of following Jesus. Like him, Alice Cooper was also a drug and alcohol user who wrestled with how to continue his career after turning to Jesus.

Lecrae told a similar story, but with different roots. He was raised in the poor black communities of Denver and learned street life including gang involvement and drugs. His idols were 2Pac, LL Cool J, and the Beastie Boys. He learned the art of rap and hip-hop at an early age, performing with friends on the streets and other gatherings from where the hip-hop culture emerged. He became a Christian in college before he was a famous rapper, and he started performing in Christian circles despite his early encounters with drugs and violence. He finally had a heart-to-heart with God in a rehabilitation institution which helped him to clarify his direction. Unlike other artists in this list, he struggled with addictions before he was famous, but used his desire to reach the culture to break solution-based rap into the world rather than the negative messages we usually encounter such as the Insane Clown Posse lyrics we examined above. Lecrae determined to create a new form of hip-hop rather than attempt to Christianize the hip-hop culture that was already spreading in America. He is certainly a man whom God is using in many ways to reach a culture many Christians do not understand how to reach[59].

THE IMPACT ON SOCIETY

We have looked at the messages the artists and producers are trying to convey to us and have also seen the results of this lifestyle on the artists themselves. It is obvious that not all artists fall over dead of drug abuse, but a large portion of them certainly have. These are the people many adults and children alike idolize and learn from. Their music and movies more often than not drip with messages contrary to what is taught in the Bible or what makes loving, honorable members of society. In light of this, it is telling to see what impact, if any, is made on society as a result of being constantly bombarded by their messages.

To illustrate, I used to work in a restaurant and in one night, all of my co-workers were running around screaming 'Timmy!' Now, my brother is a little eccentric, worked with me at the restaurant, and is named Tim, so my inclination is that he had done something to get this whole young restaurant staff wound up. After I asked him "what planet did you all visit together?" he just looked at me with disbelief and asked the casual question, "Didn't you see South Park last night?!" I discovered the program introduced the new character of Timmy, a handicapped boy that mostly just shouts his name 'Timmy!' In one night, the producers of South Park changed the vocabulary of nearly our entire staff. This change was probably not isolated to our little restaurant.

If one restaurant, and likely many more, can have their entire vocabulary, attitude, and actions changed by one thirty minute cartoon, it is not too much of a stretch to assume other messages can seep into our hearts as it has penetrated the culture. In the book, *Dancing in the Dark*, the authors observe that from the privacy of their home, children, youth, and adults alike can view media at the same time and in the same way as their peers in the neighborhoods, schools, towns and even around the country. This was first made obvious to me when I noted in my travels across the America. The various youth I visited in completely different towns all displayed the same vocabulary, and the expressions shifted unilaterally and simultaneously. Such currently popular phrases as YOLO, Cra Cra, and the like all happened simultaneously and in all regions at once. These popular expressions come, of course, from media icons. The current use of YOLO, 'you only live once' was manifested by Drake and Rick Ross[i]. They planned to do a mixed tape with the word but started a guerrilla campaign in which the phrase began showing up on T-shirts, graffiti, and other popular youth media in late 2011. The phrase took off among teenagers becoming so widespread that Drake eventually apologized for introducing it. But once an expression arises in popular culture, they remain with us for a long time.

The impact popular arts exert over consumers is not limited to word choices. I described earlier in this book about how listening to gangsta rap had shifted my language from one whom did not like to cuss into a man with a mouth like a dirty sailor. I was not an isolated incident. Lecrae said in his biographical memoirs, "My friends and I began hunting down rap videos and emulating what we saw on television. We'd sing the songs and try to replicate the outfits.[60]" He considered the rappers to be his role

---

[i] The expression was not entirely new back when it was coined by Drake and Ross. It is an alternative of *carpe diem* and the concept goes back to at least 1774 in modern history in the German play, *Clavigo*. The YOLO iteration is what we are referencing here.

models and being honest, he adopted the walking, talking, and dress of his "mentors". This is a scary prospect considering not just the revealing outfits, but even the progressive agendas surrounding many of the artists today. In movies, product placement is used as a subtle means to advertise, and even when the producer is not specifically trying to sell something, the actions the characters partake in the film can directly affect the sales of various products. Consider the sales of sunglasses. Ray-Ban's Wayfarer sunglasses were first introduced in 1956 as a revolutionary model of shades. They were popular until the 1970's, but in 1980, the glasses were worn in the classic movie *The Blues Brothers* and that year the sales spiked to 18,000 pairs in 1981. The company, still on the verge of failure, realized that placing the product in other movies would boost sales. One movie, *Risky Business*, featured the glasses and caused the sales to jump to 360,000 pairs[61]. This is a movie, not a commercial, and the sunglasses were never mentioned by name, but the star of the movie, Tom Cruise, simply placed a pair on his face.

> If a movie can sell sunglasses and staplers, it can sell sex, and sin.

By 1986 after a few more popular movies, the sales of glasses rose to 1.5 million pairs. If a movie can sell a pair of sunglasses by merely being worn by the star of the film, is it too much of a stretch to imagine the sex, drugs, alcohol consumption, profanity, and disdain for the Bible will not similarly be passed on to the viewer? All of those elements were clearly more often portrayed in *Risky Business* with a plot where the main character turned his wealthy parent's home into a whorehouse for the evening and pimping out girls to his friends. All of a sudden, the sales of sunglasses seems inconsequential. It is not a stretch to recognize that most movies, many music albums, television programs, YouTube videos, and new trends even including video games all portray acts that to actually participate in real life would prove us to be vile humans at best, and land us in jail at the worst. Is it at all possible the steady decline in morality in our society is due to the steady consumption of those terrible images? Our hearts are darkened by our sin, and that darkness pours out into society, usually with the notoriety of being displayed on the 6:00 news. After all, Rush said[62]:

> Some kind of trouble on the sensory screen
> Camera curves over caved-in cop cars
> Bleacher-creatures, would-be desperadoes
> Clutch at plausible deniability
> Don't touch that dial
> We're in denial
> Until the showcase trial on TV

> Some kind of pictures on the sense o'clock news
> Miles of yellow tape, silhouetted chalk lines
> Tough-talking hood boys in pro-team logo knock-offs
> Conform to uniforms of some corporate entity
> Don't change that station
> It's a Gangsta Nation
> Now crime's in syndication on TV

We have already argued in the last chapter that media entertainment is certainly not the exclusive cause for moral decay in our society, but we also allowed for some degree of influence. We know a cartoon can instantly change the vocabulary of an entire restaurant staff, and a youth culture can spread little catch phrases instantly across our whole country. We also examined economic data demonstrating product placement sells sunglasses, and the Insane Clown Posse is responsible for a lot of Faygo cola sales. The movie *Office Space* single-handedly made a non-existent red stapler an overnight best selling product as the company had no choice but to manufacture the famous movie prop[63]. We also know our favorite heroes sell us anything from T-shirts to macaroni and cheese, all influenced through digital media entertainment. The economy knows this because advertising is the greatest revenue stream most companies can rely on. Even Microsoft is doing away with their sales of operating systems in favor of collecting user data to market to advertisers for more revenue than they ever made from software sales. All this is because it works. The impact on society is clear: market a product, and you will sell it. Entertainment, however, does not merely sell products. The product advertising gives them a platform to produce what they are selling, and it is worldviews, it is philosophies, it is ideas. If our society at large consumes images depicting vulgar language, than such language will become a part of our society. If we begin to consume violent images and words, the fringe group in our country will act on those words. Remember the FBI classed the Juggalos as a gang because of the vast amount of violent crimes which seemed to follow the Insane Clown Posse's fan-base. Columbine copycat crimes arguably occurred because the murders were idolized on the news programs. Primetime television, even that our children watch, is full of crude humor, sexual acts, and senseless violence all for the shock value. Is it any wonder why our society is in decline? If a movie can sell sunglasses, it can sell rape. If a band can sell cola, it can sell hate. When hate, rape, violence, inconsequential sex, and callous, coarse language makes up the mental diet of our society, are we really to think the messages are merely neutral? There is a solution to all this and we will consider the solution from the mouths of some excellent artists and performers who play an active role in the limelight to help reduce the negative impact of the mainstream entertainment. What follows is how they can help.

THE GOSPEL ACCORDING TO SUPERSTARS

J ust like the rest of us, not all artists hold the same world-view over the course of their life. Some artists such as Justin Bieber and Miley Cyrus have made horrible turns for the worst casting off the 'good young star' persona for something darker, more rebellious, and sadly, more appealing to the youth they target. Other artists have seen the error of their ways and confessed Christianity as their faith. Alice Cooper was the son in a line of pastors and though diving into the deep end of dark rock, he emerged, cleaned up his ways, and professed Christianity. Brian 'Head' Welch, the former lead-man for Korn wrote an autobiography titled, *Save Me From Myself* detailing his exploits and how being a member of a raunch-band led him to a life of drugs. It was after he came to Christ that he walked away from that world and confessed Christ instead of continuing to embrace the darkness[64]. The lead guitarist of Black Sabbath wrote his own story about believing in God[65]. Several musicians and actors have turned to the light and began to preach Christ.

Two of the most vocal right now are former child-star Kirk Cameron and hip-hop artist Lecrae. Each of these artists had conversions resulting in typical 'young Christian man' behavior; they each described themselves early in their walk as *in your face* Christians preaching to people in ways perceived as generally more offensive. Please don't be concerned, it is just like an adolescent; they are growing and learning what it means to be a Christian in our world. Unfortunately, they were doing what most of our churches in America teach us to do: pray your little prayer of salvation, and then get your friends here to hear it, and then walk down the street and hand out Bible tracts! Yes, American Christianity has evolved into what looks like a multi-level marketing business, but we will tackle the solution to this problem later in this book.

Several Christian stars are living and working in Hollywood but sadly many are Christians in *profession* only. Watch the Oscars sometime and see how many people regularly use the Lord's name in vain, sing about immoral sex, and then thank Jesus for their money and awards. Fortunately, these are not the stars I am writing about here. Though Cameron and Lecrae could fall into some scandal (and I hope they do not), I have chosen to write about their particular ministries because they have taken bold stands for Jesus in theologically-thought provoking ways.

Cameron was the poster-boy teen heartthrob from the 1980's being the main character on the famous *Growing Pains* television show. He became a Christian as a 17 year old star and began growing immediately in his faith. Cameron decided to separate from the ungodly activities he was already observing in Hollywood. His years have been spent working on movies that would attempt to instill Christian values in the audience. When he is not working on movies or documentaries, he speaks to audiences in Christian circles and promotes apologetics, to encourage his audience to study the Bible and learn sound reasoning in their faith.

As a player in Hollywood, Cameron still acts and produces, but makes sure his roles do not specifically compromise his faith. Even in the popular Christian movie, *Fireproof*, he would not compromise even to the point of kissing the woman who played his wife in the film[66]. In the final kissing scene in a silhouette, the movie actually filmed his wife who came in to be a stand in for that one scene. This is a bold move in Hollywood and his general approach of taking his faith seriously is refreshing in a culture that seems to want to compromise faith for a role in film, even a role that could lead to some positive discussion.

Cameron generally takes on roles and productions trying to bring Christian apologetics to film. Some of the attempts, such as *Kirk Cameron Saving Christmas* have been laughable and incorrect on many historical merits, but nevertheless, a lot of his work, particularly with Evangelist Ray Comfort have been well thought out discussions of real issues facing many Americans, primarily students. Kirk Cameron does bring a holy light to dark Hollywood streets and we need to recognize the importance of Christian films, even if they may not be the blockbusters we find in other genres.

We have already seen a little glimpse of Lecrae's back story, but what I find more interesting is his future direction. While he started as an artist performing in Christian circles, he decided his ultimate goal is to reach the people of inner-city gang culture for Jesus. Realizing many of those kids will never attend a church and would not buy an album that was explicitly Christian, he decided to create music offering solutions to the problems in the ghetto rather than embracing the darkness present in such environments. Though many of his fans left him, negatively criticizing his closer association with main-stream hip-hop artists, Lecrae knows the only way to reach the people who need his message is to be invited to rap with the youth culture's heroes. This is exactly what Jesus did! He called Matthew out of his tax collectors booth and promptly attended a party at Matthews house with all of his friends: the tax collectors and sinners. The religious people of the day criticized Jesus and many Christians today criticize Lecrae. As far as I am concerned, he is simply doing God's work, reaching people that God placed on his heart. The Gospel is spreading in the stars.

Other artists have also contributed greatly to the cause of Christ. Skillet is another mainstream band which started as a Christian group but later went mainstream with the album *Awake*.

Even the origin of the band name, Skillet, refers to the mishmash of talents and Christian styles. They all came together, "like you put things together in a skillet" thus the band name was established. The group started by playing concerts at Christian-specific venues, but then launched out singing songs that were less explicitly about Jesus, yet the total theme, like Lecrae, is one of solutions rather than problems in the world. The song *Hero* is about the many challenges in our lives[67]:

> It's just another war
> Just another family torn
> (Falling from my faith today)
> Just a step from the edge
> Just another day in the world we live

After several verses about the problems and challenges in life, rather than leaving an empty feeling of sadness about our world, they proclaim that an answer is already here for the taking:

> Who's gonna fight for the weak
> Who's gonna make 'em believe
> I've got a hero
> Livin' in me

Several of the songs on this particular album follow similar themes: the need for a savior, the inherent sinful nature within us, and our daily struggle with living faithful lives. All Christian themes, pointing us to a savior, yet without the Christianese language that is common among more direct Christian music. Taken together, I think Skillet does excellent work with injecting some very positive messages of hope into an otherwise dark world of rock. I do not call them a Christian band; I call them a group of

Christians in a secular band – and that may be just what is needed to reach certain demographics in our modern age.

We have spent this chapter looking at the messages in our entertainment whether those be uplifting messages or not. Many artists on movie sets and band stages have an intention of passing along a sickness in their message out of either the desire to get rich or out of a need to spread their version of life. Many times these messages are not messages of hope, but every once in a while, a voice calls for positive change. Some of those messages are fabulous outcries about how we can better our lives on earth. As important as that may be, however, I am more concerned with how we live life after this earth. In the next chapter, we will examine what the Bible says about the messages we place into our minds and we will start to see a framework for how to apply the Bible to our personal entertainment choices.

CHAPTER QUESTIONS

1. If entertainment is just pleasure, why should we censor anything?

2. What is Your favorite movie? What products are in it? What lessons can be learned from it?

3. Have you ever defended an artist from a believer's criticism just because you liked their art? Did the criticism have merit?

4. What religious messages are behind the music you listen to?

5. What stars do you look up to? Have you ever examined their beliefs or lifestyle?

6. Do you use any expressions from the popular arts?

4

WHATEVER IS LOVELY, NOBLE, PURE

Finally, brethren, whatever is true, whatever is honorable, whatever is right, whatever is pure, whatever is lovely, whatever is of good repute, if there is any excellence and if anything worthy of praise, dwell on these things.
– Philippians 4:8

P*salm 119* repeats verse after verse every way possible to meditate on God's Word: memorize scripture, practice what we hear and see, pray over the words. The author repeatedly prays to God to show him His Word, teach him His ways, and even more importantly, to follow His laws. Sadly, we have forgotten the call to meditate on His precepts day and night rather favoring the latest television program, movie, or video game. Stuart McAllister observed almost all our conversation is media-centric[68]. Reflecting on that concept I found myself at a middle-school camp one summer. One of the kids in the other cabin was a friend from prior years, and I knew his dad, knowing the strong biblical root in his family. I challenged him in particular to pay close attention to the conversations he had with the kids in his cabin over the week. On the day we were packing up to go home I asked him about what he learned and he admitted nearly everything said by him and his peers did actually center around some form of popular entertainment. Likewise, think about the latest conversations with which you participated; likely they were centered around some form of entertainment production. Even in churches and small groups, fellowship dinners and even in sermons, media entertainment has become the focal point of our society.

In the previous chapter, I recounted the experience of how the South Park producers altered our restaurant staff's language in a single episode. What would happen, however, if the whole of this country professing to be Christian spent as much time in God's Word or truly serving God as they did on video games, television, movies, and the Internet? Sadder still is many professing Christians regularly entertain themselves with garbage under the guise of entertainment. What if we, whom were purchased by the blood of Christ, actually set a standard for entertainment, and what if that standard were based on some sound Biblical principles? In other words, what if Truth directed our choices in entertainment?

ORTHODOXY BASED ON TRUTH

While speaking about truth in a message series delivered to Camp of the Woods, Josh McDowell defined truth as 'fidelity to a standard'. The 'standard' used in his definition is not dictated by the local church. I can appreciate this distinction because I recently spoke to a patron at a soup kitchen who told me she could not eat meat during lent. I asked her why and she did not really know, but the church bulletin said not to eat meat on that day, so she was going to avoid it. That is scary, in fact, it is very similar to a man in Guyana who told his followers to drink Flavor Aid[i] in the guise of religious tradition resulting in over 900 people dying in one day. In fact, the very next time so many Americans perished at the same time was September 11, 2001. Under a mere religious command, many people lost their lives.

---

[i]While the old expression is "drinking the Kool-Aid", it was actually the Flavor Aid brand juice Jim Jones used to poison his many followers.

The point is clear: the church and it's leaders are not the 'standard' for truth.

While growing up, particularly in the church we are exhorted over and over to obey our parents. Old and New Testament verses exhort children to obey parents, and in the majority of matters in life, the children should indeed be obedient, but also understand parents can teach kids some really bad things. I actually had to unlearn a lot of what I learned growing up, but I am not alone. I was raised in a dysfunctional home and what I was raised to believe as normal was warped and would have led to another dysfunctional generation if I did not change my thinking. As much as we would like our parents to be the ultimate standard for truth, it just is not so. McDowell describes how many 'Christian' parents in Nazi Germany taught their children Jewish people were bad and should be killed as a result of the political ideology spreading in Germany at the time. The result was a nation practicing genocide because they were taught to believe it was right. Parents are not the 'standard' for truth.

Even the Bible itself is not the standard. Dozens of religious cults are present in this world: Jehovah's Witnesses, Mormons, Christian Science, not to mention many other smaller and less known groups. These cults all use the Bible. Sometimes they use a different translation such as the Jehovah's Witnesses, and others like the Mormons add to the Bible with extra books, but they will all use the Bible to push the congregation to submit to the church leaders. In addition to cults, many churches whom are not specifically cults and oppressive leaders, parents, and spouses use the Bible as a means to beat people into submission by pulling verses out of context and ignoring the love and truth behind the scriptures. The Bible as a collection of words is not the standard for truth.

The 'standard' is the character of God. God is truth and knowing his character will show us the way, the truth, and the life. We can understand why the Bible gets close to the standard, but the words do not make up the 'why' behind the heart. We can misread and misinterpret the Scriptures, and as the culture grows closer to the media and further from God, we have forgotten how to understand the teaching in the Bible. We need to learn the character of God, whom we meet in the pages of Scripture, but not merely by developing knowledge of a person based on a few scattered verses, but instead spending time in relationship with the creator of the universe.

Let me take this time to make a statement that will be the least controversial point in this book (at least I hope). Pornography is not something Christians should consume. Do we agree? Good! We have one thing in common. Now let's consider how that line was drawn and what is important about it. Even the hardest sinner or the newest Christian can appreciate the sexual purity of the believer. Though Christians do not always follow it, it is not a stretch to say they know purity of the believer is a good thing. Therefore, to watch pornography is an attack on purity and is something we as believers should not engage. That is a clear line, but are there other clear lines? I believe there are many and in the American culture we have a tendency to set those lines too low under the guise of freedom.

We set those lines low because of our pleasures. James writes about our interaction with the world:

> What is the source of quarrels and conflicts among you? Is not the source your pleasures that wage war in your members? You lust and do not have; so you commit murder. You are envious and cannot obtain; so you fight and quarrel. You do not have because you do not ask. You ask and do not receive, because you ask with wrong motives, so that you may spend it on your pleasures. You adulteresses, do you not know that friendship

with the world is hostility toward God? Therefore whoever wishes to be a friend of the world makes himself an enemy of God. Or do you think that the Scripture speaks to no purpose: "He jealously desires the Spirit which He has made to dwell in us"? But He gives a greater grace. Therefore it says, "God is opposed to the proud, but gives grace to the humble." Submit therefore to God. Resist the devil and he will flee from you. Draw near to God and He will draw near to you. Cleanse your hands, you sinners; and purify your hearts, you double-minded. Be miserable and mourn and weep; let your laughter be turned into mourning and your joy to gloom. Humble yourselves in the presence of the Lord, and He will exalt you (James 4:1-10).

In this section we can see our pleasures are causing our fights and they are causing us enmity with our Lord. James confronts the people with a message of repentance and humility before God. In short, be careful your pleasures are not leading you into sin. Earlier in James, he teaches us that temptation is born in our own lust, and giving into desire leads to death (*James 1:13-15*). When it comes to media entertainment, we are not happy letting God set our lines choosing instead to set our lines based on what entertains us. Think of the times someone described a movie to you and even mentions the sexual scenes, usually in embarrassment all the while justifying the bad by how entertaining the rest of the movie was.

I am not suggesting we stop watching every movie with a tiny hint of something evil, but I am suggesting we let God inform our choices. In short, let truth, as defined by consistency with God's character, become the standard for our orthodoxy, rather than letting pleasure become the standard for our orthodoxy. Orthodoxy is a theological term meaning 'right thinking' and it differs from orthopraxy, meaning 'right living'. Our living usually extends from our thinking, so it can be said orthopraxy follows orthodoxy. It is therefore important to get our thinking right so our behaviors will follow. We need to be careful of our thinking. On this matter, Paul writes in Romans:

Therefore I urge you, brethren, by the mercies of God, to present your bodies a living and holy sacrifice, acceptable to God, which is your spiritual service of worship. And do not be conformed to this world, but be transformed by the renewing of your mind, so that you may prove what the will of God is, that which is good and acceptable and perfect (Romans 12:1-2).

In this section of Scripture, Paul is telling us how to clean up our orthodoxy. First principle is to present ourselves as a living sacrifice. This means giving up desire for pleasure as the center of our life. Cast off the 'TGIF' mentality. Sure it is OK to take a break and renew yourself, but let's also glean from the wisdom of John Maxwell who said, "If you want to take a break, you have to do something first.[69]" This spiritual service of worship is to spend time with God in prayer and in the Word. The second part is to no longer be conformed to the world. Remember James says friendship with the world is hostility toward God. We have two apostles who both tell us not to conform to the world; that means we need to look at what the world does, and most of the time we should do the opposite.

Conversely, when we let our pleasures become the standard for our orthodoxy, we will gravitate toward our flesh nature and thereby reap what we have sown. Remember Paul writes:

Do not be deceived, God is not mocked; for whatever a man sows, this he will also reap. For the one who sows to his own flesh will from the flesh reap corruption, but the one who sows to the Spirit will from the Spirit reap eternal life (Galatians 6:7-8).

We all have two natures in us fighting and the one that we feed the most will dominate our life. It is for this reason we need to focus on truth and nothing else as our test of orthodoxy. If we let our emotions control us, we will let our flesh guide our entertainment and we will not look to the truths in the Scripture to guide what we watch. Conversely, we need to allow the Scriptures to guide our entertainment.

CAST OFF EVIL

I n chapter 5 we will spend more time on casting off evil, but for now, suffice it to say the epistles of Paul and the other New Testament writers do not stop at grace when using the Law to point out our sin. It has been a new attitude in the church to dwell on the fact that the law is only there to show us how good we cannot be. After all, Paul writes:

> *Therefore, my brethren, you also were made to die to the Law through the body of Christ, so that you might be joined to another, to Him who was raised from the dead, in order that we might bear fruit for God. For while we were in the flesh, the sinful passions, which were aroused by the Law, were at work in the members of our body to bear fruit for death. But now we have been released from the Law, having died to that by which we were bound, so that we serve in newness of the Spirit and not in oldness of the letter (Romans 7:4-6).*

Of course! We are not to live by the letter of the Law! The problem is modern Christians read this and swing too far toward grace. In chapter 6 we will discuss in detail the difference between licentiousness and legalism, but understand for now that forming your theology of the Law based on this section of Romans is faulty, because Paul anticipates people will come to this faulty conclusion which is why he continues in his epistle:

> *What shall we say then? Is the Law sin? May it never be! On the contrary, I would not have come to know sin except through the Law; for I would not have known about coveting if the Law had not said, "YOU SHALL NOT COVET." But sin, taking opportunity through the commandment, produced in me coveting of every*

kind; for apart from the Law sin is dead. I was once alive apart from the Law; but when the commandment came, sin became alive and I died; and this commandment, which was to result in life, proved to result in death for me; for sin, taking an opportunity through the commandment, deceived me and through it killed me. So then, the Law is holy, and the commandment is holy and righteous and good (Romans 7:7-12).

In verse 12, Paul calls the law holy, righteous, and good. It is something we do not look toward with contempt or in passing, it is something we should focus on to live a Godly life. Remember the Psalmist wrote, *"Your word I have treasured in my heart, that I may not sin against you (Psalm 119:11)."* The rest of *Psalm 119* is full of more encouragements to learn, meditate on, follow, and consider the law.

This is not just an Old Testament principle. Hebrews is a fabulous book bridging the Old Testament to the New Testament. The author writes:

For if we go on sinning willfully after receiving the knowledge of the truth, there no longer remains a sacrifice for sins, but a terrifying expectation of judgment and THE FURY OF A FIRE WHICH WILL CONSUME THE ADVERSARIES. Anyone who has set aside the Law of Moses dies without mercy on the testimony of two or three witnesses. How much severer punishment do you think he will deserve who has trampled under foot the Son of God, and has regarded as unclean the blood of the covenant by which he was sanctified, and has insulted the Spirit of grace (Hebrews 10:26-29)?

Grace is a safety net under our life that covers the fact we cannot achieve perfection, but to fail in striving to do the best we can in our Christian life is to trample underfoot the savior who paid for our sins. We cannot ever achieve perfection on earth, but we must transform our lives to live as God intends. We are not teaching a works-based salvation, but rather, our love of the Lord should lead us to follow Him in the fullness of His commandments.

Remember in many of Paul's epistles, Grace appears near the middle of the letter, not at the end. In Ephesians, it is chapter two where he records our relationship with God through faith:

But God, being rich in mercy, because of His great love with which He loved us, even when we were dead in our transgressions, made us alive together with Christ (by grace you have been saved), and raised us up with Him, and seated us with Him in the heavenly places in Christ Jesus (Ephesians 2:4-6).

The epistle does not end there with the good news of grace. Paul goes on in Ephesians 4:1 - *Therefore I, the prisoner of the Lord, implore you to walk in a manner worthy of the calling with which you have been called.* We are to cast off the evil and the old ways. *Galatians 5:25 - If we live by the Spirit, let us also walk by the Spirit.* James calls us to walk in the way of truth, not deceiving ourselves:

Therefore, putting aside all filthiness and all that remains of wickedness, in humility receive the word implanted, which is able to save your souls. But prove yourselves doers of the word, and not merely hearers who delude themselves (James 1:21-22).

The Bible is full of specific commandments to intentionally cast off evil, and these are New Testament commandments. This is not legalism, this is striving to live as our Lord has commanded us to live once we were saved by His blood.

The point is very simple. We are saved by grace through faith. Nothing else is required of us. I am not preaching a works-based Gospel. It is also true God accepts us how we are. But the old adage is all the more true: God accepts us just as we are, but He never intends to keep us there. That is why Paul wrote:

> *For I am confident of this very thing, that He who began a good work in you will perfect it until the day of Christ Jesus....And this I pray, that your love may abound still more and more in real knowledge and all discernment, so that you may approve the things that are excellent, in order to be sincere and blameless until the day of Christ; having been filled with the fruit of righteousness which comes through Jesus Christ, to the glory and praise of God (Philippians 1:6, 9-11).*

Notice the three key principles: real knowledge and discernment, approving the excellent things, and to be blameless and sincere. Even in the New Testament we are still encouraged to cast off evil and live a praiseworthy life. This means the Christian life is not an imbalanced view of grace, but a proper devotion to live as Jesus would ask us to live: *to go, and sin no more (John 8:11).*

To Grow in Christ

The verse in Philippians above contains the phrase *fruit of righteousness which comes through Jesus Christ.* Another pitfall I have observed lately is the expectation of Jesus to merely change us absent our involvement. But we do not grow in our faith apart from our involvement. Sanctification is the process where we cast off our sin and start living more like Christ in our daily life. The doctrine of sanctification includes us working on our faith and practice all the while God works in us, patching up our life where we cannot. Saint Augustine supposedly said, "Pray as though everything depended on God. Work as though everything depended on you." This is how we are to approach our sanctification: we do our very best to live in a manner worthy of our calling, but we pray God will work in our heart to take away the sins, temptations, and the pain in all of our pasts.

This does sound on the surface to be horribly legalistic, but I assure you it is really being holy which is exactly what we are called to be. This is what Peter tells us:

> Prepare your minds for action, keep sober in spirit, fix your hope completely on the grace to be brought to you at the revelation of Jesus Christ. As obedient children, do not be conformed to the former lusts which were yours in your ignorance, but like the Holy One who called you, be holy yourselves also in all your behavior; because it is written, "YOU SHALL BE HOLY, FOR I AM HOLY. (1 Peter 1:13-16)"

Surely Peter would not be commanding us to be legalistic, and he is not. We need to look at our life and determine if we are living like the unbelieving world around us, and if we are, we need to conform ourselves to the conduct of holiness.

The question remains, how do we start as people who are separated from God, living with worldly desires, and then are called to conform ourselves to Christ? Certainly as we become Christians, many people including myself report instant changes to certain aspects of our life. Outside of these changes, the rest of our life will need examination. Peter gives us further instruction in his second epistle:

> Applying all diligence, in your faith supply moral excellence, and in your moral excellence, knowledge, and in your knowledge, self-control, and in your self-control, perseverance, and in your perseverance, godliness, and in your godliness, brotherly kindness, and in your brotherly kindness, love (2 Peter 1:5-7).

This section is an implicit command to start with being diligent about our life in Christ. We understand that the power to transform our life comes from Him, but through our own efforts. In our diligence, we work on our morality, meaning we focus on conforming our actions to the will of God. This takes knowing what God has to say, what His Word says, and seeking to apply that to our life. Knowledge of the Word will lead us to learn self-control, perseverance, and godliness. Out of our godliness will come kindness and love.

In order to begin this process, we need to be a new creature. Jesus talks about the new birth in *John 3* and Paul tells us in *2 Corinthians 5* that we are a new creature in Christ. In *Romans 12*, Paul tells us to be transformed by the renewing of our mind. The intentional renewing of our mind is the first step toward growing in Christ. In our modern day, renewing our mind starts with keenly observing what we put into our head. Our entertainment is the greatest source of input. If we are always watching shows rife with sins for which our Savior died, we are not putting good, clean, noble things into our head. The sins for which I am refer can be either glorified or else used as a punch line for comedy. Getting us to laugh at sin is the first step toward us beginning to embrace it. First we laugh, then we accept it, then we approve of it, and finally we engage in sin. That is why marketers attempting to sell us products say to get the advertisement in front of the potential consumer numerous times. This also explains why many commercials are centered in comedy. Drama can sell through emotion and action can sell if your audience likes the action plot, but laughter is contagious and leads to engagement, word-of-mouth advertisement, viral videos on YouTube, and before people realize it, the product has been sold.

> In our modern day, renewing our mind starts with keenly observing what we put into our head.

Such it is with sin. We need to take a specific and conscious evaluation of what we like to do in order to entertain ourselves. Entertainment is not specifically bad, but it can be, so we must use caution. In the next several chapters we will look into exactly how to choose our entertainment, so I will not take the time to evaluate media now, just know your entertainment may be in conflict with your Christian values. Renewing your mind is the first step toward growing in Christ.

Once we have begun the process of renewing our mind by letting the Words of Christ dwell in us, our next step is to pray for God to work through us in our growth in Christ. Before Paul begins his discourse on our role in our sanctification, he starts with a prayer:

> I bow my knees before the Father, from whom every family in heaven and on earth derives its name, that He would grant you, according to the riches of His glory, to be strengthened with power through His Spirit in the inner man, so that Christ may dwell in your hearts through faith; and that you, being rooted and grounded in love, may be able to comprehend with all the saints what is the breadth and length and height and depth, and to know the love of Christ which surpasses knowledge, that you may be filled up to all the fullness of God (Ephesians 3:14-19).

When we are starting to learn how God desires us to live and we pray for Him to reveal in us His love, we start to free ourselves to follow Him fully without needing to fill our hearts with filthy entertainment. First, we must renew our minds, second, pray for strength and growth. Third, we need to start applying the commands found in the Bible to our life. Note this is not the ceremonial law found in the Old Testament. Christ came to abolish those laws, nevertheless, the New Testament is still full of commandments, what Paul calls that Law of Christ. References to this law are found in *Romans 7:25* where Paul contrasts living by the law of God verses the law of sin:

> Thanks be to God through Jesus Christ our Lord! So then, on the one hand I myself with my mind am serving the law of God, but on the other, with my flesh the law of sin.

Romans 10 clarifies righteousness is not based on our own law, but that which comes from God. Christ is the ultimate fulfillment of righteousness (*Romans 10:2-4*). It is worthy of noting at this point, to clarify again, that it is not the law which makes us right with God, it is Christ and Christ alone. Galatians repeats this point several times:

> We are Jews by nature and not sinners from among the Gentiles; nevertheless knowing that a man is not justified by the works of the Law but through faith in Christ Jesus, even we have believed in Christ Jesus, so that we may be justified by faith in Christ and not by the works of the Law; since by the works of the Law no flesh will be justified (Galatians 2:15-16).

Paul continues:

> However, the Law is not of faith; on the contrary, "HE WHO PRACTICES THEM SHALL LIVE BY THEM." Christ redeemed us from the curse of the Law, having become a curse for us (Galatians 3:12-13).

Nevertheless, he concludes the book of Galatians with an exhortation to consider what we are doing in the faith:

> Bear one another's burdens, and thereby fulfill the law of Christ. For if anyone thinks he is something when he is nothing, he deceives himself. But each one must examine his own work, and then he will have reason for boasting in regard to himself alone, and not in regard to another (Galatians 6:2-4).

There is a clear difference between the Old Testament law which we cannot fulfill on our own, and what is termed, *The Law of Christ*, as obeying the greatest of the commandments through the power of Christ in us.

Finding Entertainment in Christ

Rest

So if we are to dwell on the things that are good, noble, and pure, how are we to refresh and renew our hearts and mind? Is that even something we should do? Ultimately, our times in Christ should be deeply relaxing and refreshing to us. If it is not, pray with fervor that rest would come to us. Jesus says:

Come to Me, all who are weary and heavy-laden, and I will give you rest. Take My yoke upon you and learn from Me, for I am gentle and humble in heart, and YOU WILL FIND REST FOR YOUR SOULS. For My yoke is easy and My burden is light (Matthew 11:28-30).

Hebrews 4 and 5 discusses the believer's rest beginning with a discourse on the people of Israel as they left Egypt. The author concludes the section by declaring:

For the one who has entered His rest has himself also rested from his works, as God did from His. Therefore let us be diligent to enter that rest, so that no one will fall, through following the same example of disobedience (Hebrews 4:10-11).

It is fascinating to me that even in the statements about rest in both the Old and New Testaments, obedience is directly linked to rest.

So let us rest, rest in the knowledge of Christ that we do not need to work to earn our way into heaven. Rest in the knowledge that God has accepted us, but let us also remember rest is a recharge for doing His work. We should rest and enjoy life. We should seek Him in our times of work and our times of relaxation, so let us strive to honor Him in our entertainment. Ultimately, rest is not the end purpose of life. The TGIF mentality is not befitting of our walk in Christ, but rather, our rest should restore us to better serve His kingdom in the ways that He has prepared for us *(Ephesians 2:10)*.

ENTERTAINMENT

Any person who has lived a heathen lifestyle and then came to Christ will know of the pull between music, movies, and other entertainment choices. Sadder than that are those whom are raised in the church and cannot tell the difference because they have never considered the verses in the Bible encouraging us to walk no longer as the Gentiles walk. Remember from the beginning of this chapter our orthodoxy should be based on the Word of God, not our own pleasure and enjoyment. Let that be a factor in how we select our entertainment. In a discourse on Christian conduct, Paul writes:

> *Examine everything carefully; hold fast to that which is good; abstain from every form of evil (1 Thessalonians 5:21-22).*

This is the ultimate command. Let us look often, attentively, and intentionally at what we use to entertain ourselves. If there is a hint of evil in what we are looking at or listening to, we should desire to cast it away from us. Run to Christ as our guide for entertainment.

This chapter is meant to merely introduce the concept of dwelling on lovely things. We will not take the time to map out how to determine our entertainment yet. However, for our present purposes it is worth repeating much of what comes out of Hollywood, much of what is on the Internet, much of the music we expose ourselves to, is not lovely, pure, and noble. It is also not a wise decision to be either fully ignorant of what is out there, nor to throw out all entertainment because some of it is worthless.

In his sermon *Media: Friend or Foe*, Stuart McAllister[70] analyzes the question of whether entertainment is good or bad.

He starts the sermon suggesting media engagement is not a black or white question. Some will hope he says media is a friend since such a stance will allow movies, even vulgar ones, as sermon illustrations and so any form of entertainment is good because it is all make-believe anyway. McAllister also says some people will hope he declares media entertainment a foe. Such people want to legalistically condemn all entertainment as merely evil. Such was even our culture a few generations ago when dancing was condemned as being of the Devil. Both extremes are inappropriate and the issue is far more complex. *The basic take away from this chapter is to not dwell on media that is full of sin.* If you watch something vile, you need to decide if you will continue to engage or cut it off. Additionally, watching something once can be fine, but to watch it over and over if it glorifies sin is also a problem.

CONCLUSION

How Christians engage in media entertainment is far more important than many people believe. Those with whom we associate will determine how we behave. The biggest association of many believers is whom is in our entertainment. When we listen to a song, we are spending time with the artist. Ultimately, it is not the pleasure a song or movie gives us which is important, but the message it imposes on our life. If the song sounds great but the message is destructive, we should not listen to it because it may negatively impact our Christian walk. In other words, our orthodoxy should be determined by God's Word, not our pleasure. We are admonished in the Bible to guard what we think about, what we dwell on. Our entertainment is supposed to refresh us to get back to serving God, not an end-all to our life. Work on moving entertainment to a place that is not the end-point of our desires, but rather to refresh us to serve Christ.

CHAPTER QUESTIONS

1. Pay attention to your conversations. Are they generally focused on the popular arts?

2. Why standard do you presently use to make decisions about entertainment?

3. Why is it not appropriate to use grace as an excuse to watch anything you want regardless of content?

4. Why is it important for us to actively seek sanctification? What steps should we take first?

5. Do you find peace and rest in Christ? If not, how can you seek such rest?

WALK NO LONGER AS THE GENTILES WALK

So this I say, and affirm together with the Lord, that you walk no longer just as the Gentiles also walk, in the futility of their mind, being darkened in their understanding, excluded from the life of God because of the ignorance that is in them, because of the hardness of their heart.
– Ephesians 4:17-18

U p to this point we have discussed some philosophy from both the entertainment industry and from the Bible about monitoring our entertainment practices. This chapter is concerned with professing Christians living out their life in Christ. Paul exhorts us to daily *work out [our] salvation with fear and trembling (Philippians 2:12).* We should desire to move beyond merely calling ourselves children of God and start to live like a Christian in our general conduct, the ways we entertain ourselves, and our general attitude to life. In order to accomplish this task effectively, we need to understand the process by which people actually come to know Jesus Christ. Like all aspects of life, we do not just make a decision for Jesus and totally change everything about ourselves; we need to focus and plan our new life. We need to understand the slow process of becoming a follower of Jesus Christ. This is a crock-pot process, not a microwave procedure.

INCUBATION PERIOD

I have defined the incubation period as the time between becoming a Christian and when the new believer starts living like a Christian. We must be cognizant of the incubation period so we are not judgmental towards young believers, but we also must hold our brothers and sisters accountable for their actions. Our personal stories are varied as our DNA; each created and called by God in our own way. Billy Graham tells of a great transformation at a specific time period in his life. By contrast, his wife was raised in a Christian home and does not recall a time she did not identify as a Christian. If we spend any time in church services meeting people and inquiring of their stories, we will hear these two extremes and everything possible in between. Our story can be like Josiah. His life integrity is summarized by *2 Chronicles 34:2*:

> *He did right in the sight of the LORD, and walked in the ways of his father David and did not turn aside to the right or to the left.*

Despite his obvious dedication to the Lord, he did not always obey God's commands.

My heart resonates with this particular king in the Old Testament. Josiah's story teaches us about growing in Jesus Christ even to this day. He became king at eight years old but he did not begin to seek God until he was sixteen. Once he began to seek God for himself he did not immediately turn the kingdom back to His written commandments. *Verse 3* tells us that in the twelfth year of his kingdom when he was 20 he began turning the people back to God. What happened in those years? We are not completely sure because we know he did not have a copy of the Law. *Verse 14* says workers found the Book of the Law in the eighteenth year of his kingdom. What we do know is by either prophets, or the priest Hilkiah, or records of kingdoms past, or by personal revelation Josiah began following God. The law, discovered later, is what showed him wrath and persuaded him to repent.

We all need time to grow our faith. Some of us need to spend more time reading the Bible and learning how to apply its teachings to our life. Some of us need a little less time. None of us will come to Christ and immediately start living perfectly consistent with Christianity. This incubation period is when we grow. It is when mature believers need to help, love, and support immature believers, not allowing them to remain in immaturity, but helping them to grow in Christ.

COMING TO CHRIST IN YOUTH

M any people come to know Jesus Christ and call themselves Christian as a child or teenager. The incubation period for those coming to Christ during this life stage is very different from the growth a person experiences when coming to Christ as an adult. Many young converts will be raised in churches and homes that honor God. The natural tendency to sin is just as great as the kids from secular homes, but it can be thwarted early by loving discipline. Nevertheless, a child or teenager becoming a Christian still struggles with sin and may not look like a mature adult Christian. The family upbringing can lengthen or shorten the incubation period, depending on the level of honest communication about God and the world present in the home.

The family can shorten the incubation period of their child in several ways. The perception of the Bible is the most important factor. If the family reads the scriptures with an open heart and discusses the content regularly, the Word can directly inform the child sooner in life. The model for how we treat the Bible is found in *Deuteronomy 6*:

> *These words, which I am commanding you today, shall be on your heart. You shall teach them diligently to your sons and shall talk of them when you sit in your house and when you walk by the way and when you lie down and when you rise up.*

You shall bind them as a sign on your hand and they shall be as frontals on your forehead. You shall write them on the doorposts of your house and on your gates (6-9).

We must have great reverence and respect for what God says while avoiding vain uses of the Bible. Failure to view the Scriptures in such reverence cheapens its respect to kids. When they see the words in the sacred Scriptures do not impact our life, they do not see a reason why it should impact their life either, and the final consequence will be their living the same life as their peers while professing to be Christian, the world would never know of their salvation if left to their own actions.

In contrast, the family should seek to study the Scriptures, not as our one-verse culture has taught, but rather by devoting the whole family to the meat of the Word focusing on theology and why we believe what the Bible teaches. Sadly our world becomes so busy and focused on other outside priorities that Bible study is relocated to Sunday morning church services and youth groups which have been demonstrated to focus more on entertainment than on God or His Word.

> Service is not just something we do once in a while when nothing good is on TV, it is to be the model of the Christian life.

Next, a family can positively impact their kids by placing a high priority on relationships. A new trend in parenting is quality time. What has been forgotten is that kids spell love as T-I-M-E. Short quality time is not as important as spending more time with our kids, but most ideal is time that is both quality and quantity. It is not enough to merely spend some time with your kids; learn to talk to them as well. Seek to understand their world-view and ask questions often; non-judgmentally get into their world. Kids and teenagers need different approaches to conversation but they are both more than willing to talk to an adult who will listen.

Talking is not enough, however, we need to look at how we talk to our kids. One insight was recently explained to me by a teenager: there is a difference between talking *at* your child and talking *with* your child. The difference is when a parent is talking at their children, the assumption is the parent is completely correct, and the conversation comes off as barking orders and failing to connect. While barking orders may be a great approach to handle a six-year old, a sixteen-year old requires more respect. Talking with the sixteen-year old however looks a whole lot more like a dialog where parents allow themselves to be instructed by their kids, and that requires humility on behalf of the parents. This is the conversation style in mind with the old adage: People do not care what you know until they know that you care.

Finally, service will decrease the incubation period for our kids. We are called out of our life of sin to the kingdom of peace to serve mankind. *Ephesians 2:10* reminds us that:

> *We are His workmanship, created in Christ Jesus for good works, which God prepared beforehand so that we would walk in them.*

Service is not just something we do once in a while when nothing good is on TV, it is to be the model of the Christian life. Including our kids in the services we render to other people will show them we truly commit to serving the Lord, and thus, will show our kids a God who is real. Once they know the Lord is real, they will take seriously the things of the kingdom.

We help our kids out best by serving in the kingdom. Our goal is not that our kids become little self-righteous soldiers inviting everyone to church, but rather the goal is for them to live out their salvation humbly serving other people in the same love Jesus showed us. The best way for them to do that is to usher them through the incubation period by living as the Word teaches. We must know the Word and treat it reverently. In addition, we need to include our kids in our life, and let them include us in theirs. Spend time that is both quality and quantity and certainly include them in the services we render to our fellow citizens.

COMING TO CHRIST AS AN ADULT

M any people come to know Jesus Christ as an adult, and in our current culture, that means many of us coming to Christ as an adult may have never heard the wonderful hymns which 'everyone knows'. It is true, *Amazing Grace* was a totally new song to me when I was an adult, but sin was more real to me than it was to my peers whom were raised in the church. Ultimately, we need to be more cognoscente about the residual knowledge of Christians we encounter.

As someone who came late to Christ, I had lived a worthless life before God. To be sure, we late bloomers have certain areas of sin we would never tread, like a self-righteous root or a deeply-planted seed waiting to sprout. For me, drugs was off-limits, rejected as being completely stupid. But my pride in academia was an area of sin for which I was totally blind. Many come to Christ after a brush with the law, or as a result of fighting through addictions. Still others come to Christ painfully limping along. As I once wrote in a poem:

> What I see in the garden is pain, enough that without Your
> comfort, would drive me insane
> I see the hearts, soiled and crying, laden with death,
> alone and dying

Many adults are on the verge of insanity, using pills to fight depression, and seeking anything to fill the hole in their heart only to hit bottom. Finally in a desperate cry for help they call to the One who could save them all along. We people are so prideful we need to hit that bottom before we crawl out of the trash heap and into the loving arms of God.

Our incubation period lasts much longer in many cases. If we are addicted to drugs when we meet Jesus, we need to fight an addiction parallel to learning about our savior. We might have come to Christ in desperation from a failed marriage, and we turn to God for comfort as we seek out building a new life. Some of us come from prison and need to learn how to live in this world apart from crime. Many more stories and struggles could be told, and add to those the task of learning about God means more time in the incubation period is frequently needed.

Though it is true more time in the incubation period is needed for us, it is not always the case for the simple reason some of us have lost so much that we have nothing more to cling onto than the hand of God whom will never let us go (John 10). In my desperation, I spent so much time listening to sermons, reading the Bible and books about the Bible, praying and thinking that it took me about four years to overcome my major hurdles. I still deal with sin, but as time grows on I am focused more and more on Christ and my life starts to reflect His character.

The ultimate key to reducing the incubation period of coming late in life to Christ is the time we spend with God. No matter our sins, addictions, pains, struggles, we can find hope and help in the loving arms of God through it all, and the more we reach out to Him, the sooner we come to Him. James says:

Draw near to God and He will draw near to you. Cleanse your hands, you sinners; and purify your hearts, you double-minded. Be miserable and mourn and weep; let your laughter be turned into mourning and your joy to gloom. Humble yourselves in the presence of the Lord, and He will exalt you (James 4:8-10).

One sermon a week and a social get-together with Christians is not enough to draw near to God; we need to bathe in the Word daily with a clear focus of learning who He is. We need to learn about God from dedicated pastors, and we need to daily challenge our life, only then do we crawl through the incubation period.

READ AND APPLY THE SCRIPTURES

B arna polls revealed only 19% of Christians actually read their Bibles and for the first time ever, the number of people in America who are skeptical of the Bible is equal to those whom are engaged with the Good Book. If the current relation to those numbers is not sad enough, the trend should cause weeping in the church since people skeptical of the Scriptures are increasing and the number of people engaged in the Bible is in sharp decline. We as the Church in America are responsible for this trend. These numbers are related to the fact that we spend less time in the Scriptures, so the Bible becomes more and more irrelevant to the next generation.

To complicate the matter, we choose to spend far more on entertainment every month than we do on any form of Christian service or ministry. I am not saying to give more money or time to the church, but rather, to help, serve, and use your resources to better the kingdom. In light of this, as we spend more on entertainment and engage in more entertainment, we are setting the precedent for our next generation that entertainment is more important than Christian service. We even disguise our addiction to entertainment as 'fellowship'. If, however, we look at the entertainment, we see the general themes running throughout the popular arts are hostile toward God. Many of the messages are to follow your heart, whatever you feel is right, and even that the Bible is an old, irrelevant collection of writers who were stoned out on mushrooms. Such is the culture for which our kids are being raised, and it is the culture we have allowed into our life, our mind, our personal lifestyle. Like it or not, it impacts our world view.

The key to positive change when we want to shift our lifestyle is first to add good habits. Here we add Scripture including sermons, both fast and deep Bible study, and fellowship with other believers which includes discussing the Word. We are adding a heavy dose of prayer to our lives. I want to focus first on adding to our current lifestyle because to remove our old habits while simultaneously adding new generally results in failure. It happens with diet, budgeting, education, and even our growth in Christ. Start by adding a few minutes in the morning and evening to reading the Bible or praying. Find a Christian station that will broadcast sermons and spend some time in the car listening to good preachers. You can also download many sermons for free or find some good ministries and request to be placed on their resources mailing list to receive books and sermons. These small additions to your current lifestyle will slowly get you used to listening and thinking about the Bible, and that is the beginning for our understanding God's law.

With the slow addition to Bible teaching in our life, we let the Spirit act to inform us on when and how to remove things from our life. Recall from the previous chapter we should not base our entertainment decisions on our pleasures or feelings, but rather, to let the Bible be our guide. Let the Word of God speak about removing bad habits, bad stations, and bad movies we formerly took pleasure in engaging. With newer habits of Bible study and prayer starting to take root, we slowly remove things drawing us away from the Lord.

While our next chapter will provide a much better concise set of guidelines for entertainment, we can get a primer by examining some verses in Scripture and testing those against movies, music, YouTube videos, or other entertainment we use to amuse ourselves. David says in *Psalm 101, I will set no worthless thing before my eyes.* An alternate rendering might say to *set no apostasy before ourselves.* David had a keen focus of what was good to see and what was not, and if there was any question about the impact of visual stimulation before Bathsheba, David certainly knew the power of even quick peeks after his adulterous act, for the great sin happened when he *saw* her bathing (*2 Samuel 11:2*).

What we see stirs up feelings and emotions in our life for better or worse. Though David had many wives and concubines he could have summoned at a moment's notice, seeing this one woman caused him to forget about all else. This is the true danger in looking at pornography, for one look can stir up emotions in us leading to addiction lasting a lifetime and causing a wake of destruction in its path. So it is with viewing violence, vulgarity, or sin in general. As comedy, first we laugh at it, then we joke about it ourselves, then we cautiously dip our toe into it, and before long we embrace a sin as our habit and only see the horrible consequences in retrospect. This is the subtle effect of media entertainment. We must be very careful what we watch, and how we watch it.

A quick evaluation can be drawn between the Bible and our entertainment from two lists found in Galatians. Many who have been raised in the church will be familiar with the fruit of the spirit found in *Galatians 5:22-23: love, joy, peace, patience, kindness, goodness, faithfulness, gentleness, self-control.* Another list comprised of sinful attitudes is also found in the same chapter (*19-21*):

Immorality, impurity, sensuality, idolatry, sorcery, enmities, strife, jealousy, outbursts of anger, disputes, dissensions, factions, envying, drunkenness, carousing, and things like these.

Just have a look at these two lists. If our entertainment better resembles the second list we may be better off finding another movie to watch, song to listen to, or game to play.

Paul expands more on the topic of how to live holy in the book of Ephesians, particularly in the fourth and fifth chapters. In *chapter 4:17-19*, Paul writes:

So this I say, and affirm together with the Lord, that you walk no longer just as the Gentiles also walk, in the futility of their mind, being darkened in their understanding, excluded from the life of God because of the ignorance that is in them, because of the hardness of their heart; and they, having become callous, have given themselves over to sensuality for the practice of every kind of impurity with greediness.

Just look at the lineup of modern television shows and you will see these attitudes expressed over and over. Consider whether watching those attitudes will help you or hinder you as you seek to grow in Christ, or even better, if engaging with these attitudes is contrary to your love for Jesus.

Paul spends the remainder of the fourth chapter of Ephesians exhorting the Christians of Ephesus to live in a manner worthy of being called Christians, but in the fifth chapter he carries the discussion further encouraging the believers to not even associate with such people. *Ephesians 5:6-10* says:

Let no one deceive you with empty words, for because of these things the wrath of God comes upon the sons of disobedience. Therefore do not be partakers with them; for you were formerly darkness, but now you are Light in the Lord; walk as children of Light (for the fruit of the Light consists in all goodness and righteousness and truth), trying to learn what is pleasing to the Lord.

As Christians, we need to break away from such things whether they be actual sinful actions or the comedy and glorification of such conduct in the form of media entertainment. *Verse 11* says we should not only avoid participation in sinful deeds, but that we should expose them for evil as well.

As Christians, we should be salt and light. That is the phrase that Jesus uses in the Sermon on the Mount (*Matthew 5:13-16*):

> *You are the salt of the earth; but if the salt has become tasteless, how can it be made salty again? It is no longer good for anything, except to be thrown out and trampled under foot by men.*

> *You are the light of the world. A city set on a hill cannot be hidden; nor does anyone light a lamp and put it under a basket, but on the lampstand, and it gives light to all who are in the house. Let your light shine before men in such a way that they may see your good works, and glorify your Father who is in heaven.*

Salt is a preservative used for preventing foods from going rancid. Jesus tells us here that we have responsibility in our culture to preserve it from the negative impact of sin. We are to be the salt that prevents the culture from going into total chaos so we have setup schools, hospitals, and met physical needs of the world. Without the Christians here to keep the culture in check, total evil and disorder would overtake us, and the increasing trend toward such things is reflective of the fact we, as the American church, are taking our Bibles less seriously. We have become tasteless and are now being trampled under the feet of post-modernism, LGBT ideology, atheism, and other sins popularized in modern media.

The purpose of light is to show the way. Just like Moses' face shown with the Glory of God after his extended stay on Mount Sinai (*Exodus 24*), our face should shine with the Glory of Jesus and we should always be ready to prepare a defense for the hope residing within us (*1 Peter 3:15*). Our light has been dimmed and our faces bear the problems of the world instead of the solution found in Christ. Rather than being able to point people to the Savior, we can usually only point them to a church, and that does not usually mean salvation in this culture. We need to know the Word better ourselves so we can lead people to Christ and not rely on the Pastor to 'convert' our friends.

Since we are impacted by what we see and hear, we need to guard our input and focus instead on understanding the Bible. When we take time for recreation, we should be evaluating our entertainment to make sure it is not glorifying sins for which our Savior died. Use the Scriptures as a guide, but our next chapter will go into greater detail about the verses and philosophy of God-honoring entertainment.

PLEADING TO THE INDIVIDUAL

Our faith is personal. I am hesitant to say our faith must solely be our own lest we forget our upbringing in the Lord was affected by our spiritual parents. As we were conceived in this physical body, we were dependent on the food our mother ate. We know a pregnant woman who drinks or abuses drugs will give birth to a child addicted to drugs or having a developmental condition. Likewise, a conscientious mother will watch every aspect of her environment to protect the body growing inside her. Once we were born, we were not left to fend for ourselves in this hostile world, but instead were clothed, fed, and protected. We then develop a relationship with our parents. As we learn to walk and talk our parents are there to clean up the bruises, correct the words, and help us grow into the person we are meant to be.

Such it is with a child in the faith. Our faith is our own, but only after it grows. We are nurtured by trusting parents in the Lord. What our parents spiritually eat while we are growing will have a role in deciding our spiritual DNA. As we start walking on our own, we will be guided and directed by spiritual parents keeping an eye on us. They do not want us to eat spiritual poison, though they will allow us to develop our own tastes and to guide us. That is how Christians are born and developed. We need mentoring in the faith, and only after we go through our spiritual growth spurts are we ready to tackle the challenges of a pagan world which the Holy Spirit has came to affront.

So, yes, our faith is our own...but yes, our faith is affected and influenced by our mentors. We may need a mentor now. We may need to make some specific changes in our own life. I plead with the American church to develop our faith by learning the Word under the direction of spiritual parents. Do you think you have a strong faith, know the Word, and apply it regularly to your life? Great! Mentor someone in that faith. This is how we will start to make changes in our own lives bringing glory to God.

The ultimate goal for us as individuals is to make decisions about our life, health, entertainment, and finances that bring glory to God and help us in our own good works for the kingdom of heaven. Remember to store up your treasures in heaven where the moth does not eat nor thieves break in and steal (*Matthew 6:19*). You can achieve this end by casting aside the old life and seeking the new life in Christ. This applies to those who come to Christ late in life, but it also applies to those coming to faith as a child or teenager. If you are reading this in your youth, make good decisions for yourself, not based on rules from your parents, but rather on obedient love for Jesus Christ. If you are an adult reading this, take stock of your options for entertainment now and do something about any changes that need to be made.

INDIVIDUALS MAKE UP THE CHURCH

My high school chemistry teacher taught me a great (non-chemical) lesson: *We are only as safe as the least safe person.* The principle has to do with the weakest part of the chain and can be broadly expressed in many areas. Adjusted for the church, it might say *we are only as strong as the least strong person.* The church is a collection of people who collectively make up the body of Christ. We can argue if we are talking about the physical congregation or the Church Universal, but that does not matter for now. The bottom line is if we attend a church, we are part of the body of Christ, and our service is needed. Not necessarily for the advertised ministry needs (though that is a valid part of service). We are all designed with our own gifts, passions, and personality. We all need to do our part. Paul writes:

> For even as the body is one and yet has many members, and all the members of the body, though they are many, are one body, so also is Christ. For by one Spirit we were all baptized into one body, whether Jews or Greeks, whether slaves or free, and we were all made to drink of one Spirit (1 Corinthians 12:12-13).

Though each of us is our own person, we collectively build the church. If the individual members of the church are weak in Christ, spend their time in media that fails to glorify God, and have a poor comprehension of the Bible, the church itself will be weak and ineffective. I believe this is why more kids leave church as they grow up, more people are skeptical of the Bible, and fewer people are truly engaged in the Scriptures.

To contrast the weak church, Paul continues:

Now you are Christ's body, and individually members of it. And God has appointed in the church, first apostles, second prophets, third teachers, then miracles, then gifts of healings, helps, administrations, various kinds of tongues. All are not apostles, are they? All are not prophets, are they? All are not teachers, are they? All are not workers of miracles, are they? All do not have gifts of healings, do they? All do not speak with tongues, do they? All do not interpret, do they? But earnestly desire the greater gifts. And I show you a still more excellent way (1 Corinthians 12:27-31).

One of the great strengths of a fully functioning mature church is mentors arise to help the young believers in natural relationships, not forced programs. Furthermore, leadership can spot weaker segments in their body and seek to strengthen them with doctrine. If you happen to be a church leader reading this, do not merely seek to place new members into Sunday school classes or small groups, but make sure everyone has a mentor. Be sensible some parishioners have mentors outside of your church or your leadership, and that is OK as long as they are being mentored in sound principles. Have a plan in place for mentoring that is not problematically assigned, but mutually agreed upon; real teaching leading to growth cannot be forced.

If you are new to the faith of Jesus Christ, you need a mentor to strengthen you. If you were led to Christ by someone, they should generally help to mentor you if possible, and if you determine they are suitable to do so. If you do not have someone who can serve as your mentor in Christ, ask the pastor of your church for a recommendation to find a mentor. Interview a few people and spend some time before making the final decision on who mentors you since some people are simply not compatible. In this, the final goal is your growth in Christ.

We should be earnestly seeking God in our life, seeking the works He has appointed for us, seeking Him at all times, not just inside (or outside) entertainment. Since our church is built from a collection of the individual members, the church becomes weaker as the members are weaker, and the church becomes stronger as the members are stronger. In light of this, we should seek to find God in all areas of our life, including our entertainment. We should make better decisions in our life to prioritize time with God. When we do this as a collective church community, we gain the strength to resist the evil one and survive this cultural storm.

CHAPTER QUESTIONS

1. Was there a time in your life you were not a Christian? What was your salvation experience like?

2. How long was your Incubation Period?

3. Relatively speaking, what is the ratio of Christian participation to popular entertainment in your life?

4. Do you have a spiritual mentor? Are you mentoring someone in the faith?

5. Why do spiritually immature believers hurt the church? How can we strengthen the church with our sanctification?

6

OBSERVING THE GUARDRAILS

Therefore I, the prisoner in the Lord, exhort you to walk in a manner worthy of the calling with which you have been called.
- Ephesians 4:1

Our modern Christian era has seen an increase in bickering between believers around the question of morality. To some believers, Jesus came to set us free from sin and he did just that. In their mind, there is no further discussion or burden on us. After all, Jesus did say: *For My yoke is easy and My burden is light (Matthew 11:30)*. So how can we possibly ask people to conform to any view less than giving total freedom in all things in Jesus. But to other believers, the mere idea we do not look at our lifestyle when we become believers is heresy. Jesus even agrees with this when He said to a man he healed one Sabbath, *Behold, you have become well; do not sin anymore, so that nothing worse happens to you (John 5:14)*. How can we as sinners come to Jesus and not change our lifestyle? This chapter will examine what the Scriptures have to say about the legalities involved in living the Christian life.

LEGAL TROUBLES

When the Israelites left Egypt, God delivered the Ten Commandments through Moses as the basis for their living with Him. The book of Leviticus further describes the laws God required the Israelites to remember and practice in their daily lives. By the time of Jesus, Pharisees reduced the law to a huge set of rules the Jewish people generally had to obey, and as Jesus preached many times, they forgot about their God and His reasons behind His law. The Pharisees essentially began to worship the law itself. This deep focus on the law lends to the condition called Legalism.

While being a legalist is not a good thing, it is an overused phrase. Chip Ingram said in a sermon at one point that many people are too quick to brand others as legalist when they are merely living as God commands. **Legalism is not to be obedient to God, but rather, to worship the law as the means to salvation.** The sacrifice Jesus gave us on the cross did not abolish the holy living God requires of His people. Jesus said He did not come to abolish the law, but to fulfill it. He then declares anyone who minimizes the law will be called least in the Kingdom but those who teach the law will be called the greatest in the Kingdom (*Matthew 5:17-19*). We see here the law is not a means to salvation, but something to take seriously in our daily walk with God.

The opposite extreme to legalism is called Antinomianism, a compound word in Greek meaning 'against the law' or 'without law'. **Thus, an antinomianist is a person who believes there are no binding laws and all things are legal for the Christian.** To this person, we are totally free in Christ because He died for our sins and thus, removed the sting of death and the consequence of sin. This person may cite a verse we will examine in detail later in this chapter: *All things are lawful for me, but not all things are profitable (1 Corinthians 6:12).*

As the Christian faith began to spread throughout the world, a debate broke out between the Jewish and Gentile believers. Peter became the apostle called to reach out to the Gentiles in response to prayer from Cornelius, a Gentile centurion.

God had to challenge Peter's prejudices and did so in the following way:

Peter went up on the housetop about the sixth hour to pray. But he became hungry and was desiring to eat; but while they were making preparations, he fell into a trance; and he saw the sky opened up, and an object like a great sheet coming down, lowered by four corners to the ground, and there were in it all kinds of four-footed animals and crawling creatures of the earth and birds of the air. A voice came to him, "Get up, Peter, kill and eat!" But Peter said, "By no means, Lord, for I have never eaten anything unholy and unclean." Again a voice came to him a second time, "What God has cleansed, no longer consider unholy." This happened three times, and immediately the object was taken up into the sky (Acts 10:9-16).

God was using this perplexing situation to prepare Peter for interacting with Gentiles, and it worked. Cornelius's men found Peter right where God told them he would be. We read further:

While Peter was reflecting on the vision, the Spirit said to him, "Behold, three men are looking for you. But get up, go downstairs and accompany them without misgivings, for I have sent them Myself (Acts 10:19-20)."

Peter realizes this message is from God, so he went with the men. Upon meeting Cornelius, he said:

You yourselves know how unlawful it is for a man who is a Jew to associate with a foreigner or to visit him; and yet God has shown me that I should not call any man unholy or unclean. That is why I came without even raising any objection when I was sent for. So I ask for what reason you have sent for me (Acts 10:28-29).

This is the first recorded interaction between the Jewish Christians and the Roman Gentiles, but there was conflict moving forward. It was Paul who truly began to spread the Gospel among the Gentiles. However, the Jewish believers in the towns who worshiped with the Gentiles started to assume Christians, coming from a Jewish Messiah, were bound to follow the Mosaic law. Paul brings that question before the apostles in Jerusalem and we get a response in *Acts 15*:

> *Since we have heard that some of our number to whom we gave no instruction have disturbed you with their words, unsettling your souls, it seemed good to us, having become of one mind, to select men to send to you with our beloved Barnabas and Paul, men who have risked their lives for the name of our Lord Jesus Christ. Therefore we have sent Judas and Silas, who themselves will also report the same things by word of mouth. For it seemed good to the Holy Spirit and to us to lay upon you no greater burden than these essentials: that you abstain from things sacrificed to idols and from blood and from things strangled and from fornication; if you keep yourselves free from such things, you will do well. Farewell (Acts 15:24-29).*

We see here the Jewish law is not specifically binding on the Gentiles, so does that mean there is no binding law on Christians today? Paul addresses this very question in the book of Romans. He is describing sin's entrance into the human race through one man, Adam, but it was another man, Jesus, who paid the penalty of our sin (*Romans 5:12-18*). Paul continues saying the greater our sin, the greater the grace we received which saved us. This is in perfect alignment with what Jesus said about the woman who was washing His feet with her tears through the parable of the two debtors:

> *"A moneylender had two debtors: one owed five hundred denarii, and the other fifty. When they were unable to repay, he graciously forgave them both. So which of them will love him more?" Simon answered and said, "I suppose the one whom he forgave more." And He said to him, "You have judged correctly." Turning toward the woman, He said to Simon, "Do you see this woman? I entered your house; you gave Me no water for My feet, but she has wet My feet with her tears and*

wiped them with her hair. You gave Me no kiss; but she, since the time I came in, has not ceased to kiss My feet. You did not anoint My head with oil, but she anointed My feet with perfume. For this reason I say to you, her sins, which are many, have been forgiven, for she loved much; but he who is forgiven little, loves little (Luke 7:41-47)."

Paul probably had this story in mind when he asked and answered the rhetorical question in *Romans 6:*

Are we to continue in sin so that grace may increase? May it never be! How shall we who died to sin still live in it (vs 1-2)?

It is clear though the Mosaic law is not binding on us, something of the law is certainly binding as evidenced by almost every book in the New Testament. In this chapter, we will examine the Christian commands found in the New Testament.

GRAY AREA DECISIONS

As Paul echoes, *May it never be* in the verse above, he is addressing here the interplay between sin and grace. The greater the sin, the greater the grace. Samuel rebuked Saul as the king who failed to carry out the command to completely destroy the Amalekites, the prophet said:

Has the Lord as much delight in burnt offerings and sacrifices as in obeying the voice of the Lord? Behold, to obey is better than sacrifice, and to heed than the fat of rams. For rebellion is as the sin of divination, and insubordination is as iniquity and idolatry. Because you have rejected the word of the Lord, He has also rejected you from being king (1 Samuel 15:22-23).

Clearly, God is concerned with our obedience and the New Testament is full of commands, but not every aspect in our life is prescribed, and some things may be sin to one person, but not sin to another *(James 4:17).* This is where the idea of gray area decisions comes into play. For example, the Bible does not say drinking alcohol is necessarily a sin, but if we use our freedom to drink in the presence of a brother who was an alcoholic and we tempt him back into his drunken way, we have caused our brother to stumble, and in the words of Jesus, it would be better for us if we had a millstone hung around our neck and we be cast into the sea (*Matthew 18:6*).

Gray areas are life decisions that do not have a specific command in Scripture. It is pretty clear from both the Old and the New Testament we should not engage in sexual immorality, nor idolatry. We also have specific commands about obeying authority, putting God first in all aspects of our life, but many areas of life do not have a direct commandment, though many people may wish it were so. In an interview between John MacArthur and Philip Johnson, MacArthur said that he wished the Bible was more clear on topics such as divorce and drinking. I would add entertainment and other cultural mores such as body modifications and the like, but we just do not have our life prescribed and probably for good reason. Regardless, Paul does give us reflections about gray area decisions in two of his epistles, so we will examine those in turn.

My first principle in gray area decision making is to never go against your conscience.

He describes gray area decisions as a matter of the conscience. *Romans 14* deals specifically with our need to listen to our conscience. I believe the Spirit works as a megaphone to our inherent morals, and even though we may have desensitized our conscience throughout our life as a sinner, God can restore and amplify our inner voice. My first principle in gray area decision making is to never go against your conscience. If you have a weird feeling about a matter, slow down and gather more facts. Remember a part of grace is some people may have freedoms you do not and vice versa, but each of us should never do something that we do not feel right about. In *Romans 14*, Paul writes:

> *I know and am convinced in the Lord Jesus that nothing is unclean in itself; but to him who thinks anything to be unclean, to him it is unclean (verse 14).*

Paul makes the point in Romans several times by explaining the origin of this principle: it is possible we have come from a background that makes something sin or like sin. As an example, I came from a background submerged in heavy metal and I personally witnessed many of the sinful behaviors rampant in that culture. For a long time as a weaker brother in the faith, I would see any association of heavy metal as sin due to the association with the metal culture. As such, some of the new 'Christian' heavy metal would become a sin problem in my life, and we need to take that into consideration when we are deciding if such music is really an important part of our churches, youth groups, and in the company of other believers whom we may not know very well. On this point, Paul writes:

> *Accept the one who is weak in faith, but not for the purpose of passing judgment on his opinions. One person has faith that he may eat all things, but he who is weak eats vegetables only. The one who eats is not to regard with contempt the one who does not eat, and the one who does not eat is not to judge the one who eats, for God has accepted him (Romans 14:1-3).*

Ultimately, we need to live out our life in faith, not in sin. Paul concludes *Romans 14* by writing:

> *He who doubts is condemned if he eats, because his eating is not from faith; and whatever is not from faith is sin (verse 23).*

My second principle in gray area decisions is to consider the other believers. While it is very true we have a lot of freedom in Jesus (*1 Corinthians 8:4-6*), our freedom does not grant us total right to do what we want in all circumstances. Paul writes:

> *But take care that this liberty of yours does not somehow become a stumbling block to the weak. For if someone sees you, who have knowledge, dining in an idol's temple, will not his conscience, if he is weak, be strengthened to eat things sacrificed to idols? For through your knowledge he who is weak is ruined, the brother for whose sake Christ died. And so, by sinning against the brethren and wounding their conscience when it is weak, you sin against Christ. Therefore, if food causes my brother to stumble, I will never eat meat again, so that I will not cause my brother to stumble (1 Corinthians 8:9-13).*

We need to consider our weaker brothers when we are making choices in the gray areas. If what we eat, what we listen to, what we watch, what we play are objectionable to our weaker brothers, we must abstain so we do not do damage to the cause of Christ. This is a very applicable section of scripture as we consider our entertainment. Obviously as we shall see, some media entertainment is not for believer's eyes, but other forms of entertainment can be acceptable if we understand the liberties we have in Jesus. Each person must make up his or her own mind as they consider the scriptures when they are seeking to make decisions in media entertainment. Never go against your conscience, and never go against the conscience of believers presently with you. Remember the weaker brother is to be considered, and our churches, sadly, are full of weaker brothers and sisters.

IN ENTERTAINMENT

T he question of entertainment in the life of the Christian is one rife with debate. Stuart McAlliester began his sermon on *Media: Friend or Foe* by listing the two extremes: some people will want to conclude media is a friend. These people want to be told any level of entertainment is fine with the Christian because first, we are redeemed by the blood of Christ, and secondly it is all just fake anyway. Other people would want to conclude media is a foe; a pure distraction to the things of Christ and certainly not worthy of a Christian's partaking[71]. The real answer: it is not black and white and we are not commanded one direction or another on media entertainment as a whole, which makes this a gray area decision.

In order to go about determining whether a particular piece of media entertainment is appropriate for our Christian life, we need to examine it carefully. Some programs are easy to determine and may even be directed to a specific commandment. In *Psalm 101*, David writes:

> *I will set no worthless thing before my eyes;*
> *I hate the work of those who fall away;*
> *It shall not fasten its grip on me.*
> *Psalm 101:3*

What is worthless for a Christian? It is a program glorifying sex outside the constraints of marriage, or one making light of God or His Word. It is a song screaming God is dead and Satan is king. It is a website distributing pornography or a video game glorifying anarchy, prostitution, or any other clearly defined Biblical sins. These forms of entertainment are clearly worthless and they are the works of those who have fallen away or have never known the King to begin with. Ultimately, the way we want to make right decisions about our media entertainment is to know the Bible and decide to live by it. But it is more complicated than that as we shall see in our chapter on examining everything carefully.

Obviously to any remotely mature Christian, pornography is off the table for an entertainment choice, but how do we handle movies with R ratings, sexual scenes, jokes, murders, drugs, godlessness, and rebellion? Why is it some Christians feel justified in watching programs like Family Guy while others look toward such programs with disdain? All this depends on where you set the standard, the bar by which you personally use to determine where you cross the line. I sadly fear many professing Christians let their pleasures set the bar instead of letting God set standards for entertainment. In other words, **we allow our pleasure to determine our orthodoxy instead of letting sound theology determine our orthodoxy**. The end result is a church who thinks Family Guy is OK because it is 'funny satire' or a 'humorous take on our culture' but South Park is just 'vile'. However, these statements seem to be based on taste in personal entertainment value of the person making the judgment. Instead of letting the pleasure determine if you watch something for entertainment, we should instead examine everything through the lens of the scriptures.

The principle is found in *1 Thessalonians 5:21-22*:

> *Examine everything carefully; hold fast to that which is good; abstain from every form of evil.*

This is not just a little phrase included in the New Testament in order to make an inspirational social media meme, but it is in a section of the letter discussing Christian conduct. Paul is writing about general life conduct. In everything we do be it spiritually, physically, for our work or for our relaxation, examine everything carefully. Hold fast to that which is good and abstain from every evil thing. Remember your conscience is your guide, so that means we cannot just let our pastor or our favorite talk show host be our guide. We must personally take the intentional effort to examine our life. Socrates said the unexamined life is not worth living. I agree. We must examine our life so we do not fall prey to people who would lead us astray. Jesus likewise encouraged us to examine the life and message of those who teach us:

> Beware of the false prophets, who come to you in sheep's clothing, but inwardly are ravenous wolves. You will know them by their fruits. Grapes are not gathered from thorn bushes nor figs from thistles, are they? So every good tree bears good fruit, but the bad tree bears bad fruit. A good tree cannot produce bad fruit, nor can a bad tree produce good fruit. Every tree that does not bear good fruit is cut down and thrown into the fire. So then, you will know them by their fruits (Matthew 7:15-20).

Though Jesus is speaking specifically about teachers, Paul is encouraging us through a similar principle to examine everything about our life, not just the teachers or the entertainment. Filter everything through the Scriptures and make decisions on all aspects of life based on what the Bible teaches us about living. We are not looking for specific verses like "Thou shall not watch this program..." We are instead looking for overarching, guiding principles on our life through difficult and dedicated study.

EVER-PRESENT EVIL

The age-old question is how an all-powerful and good God would allow evil in the world. I do not believe this is as difficult a question as some may think, nor does it require a cop-out to say "God's ways are above our ways." The reality is evil is in the world because Adam and Eve sinned, but God allows evil in the world because without evil, love is meaningless.

The existence of evil in our world lets us see the conflict between good and evil. Our response to evil tells us more about our condition than it does about the state of the world. I can live in this world, see the evil, and love God all the more. Our love for God should direct us to stray from the glorification of sin found in many sectors of the entertainment industry. We need to ask ourselves why is it we like blood, violence, sex, drunkenness, and the like in the programming we watch. Are we more attracted to the evil than we are the good? Is it possible that if God would simply wipe out all of the evil in this world, He might just take us all out as it was in the days of Noah?

In reality, God declares in Genesis after the floodwaters subsided that He would never again wash away the whole world in a flood. That is good news until we get to that part in *2 Peter* where the Bible says the world is reserved for fire! But that notwithstanding, God did act on the world and He still does act in the world in response to sin. The Bible speaks of sins upon sins, but some are far more common in the human condition. After the exile from Eden, murder was the first recorded sin, possibly only behind jealously since Cain murdered Abel because God considered the latter sacrifice better, but before the first book of the Bible is complete, we have seen jealousy and murder, sexual sin of all kinds, oppression and thievery. The wonderful world created by our awesome God was made destitute by the sins of the people who were supposed to be stewards of all creation. Even today, many companies and governments think nothing of pillaging the land for their gain only to leave a wake of destruction in their path. These are the sins in our world, and they are the sins our tainted human hearts gravitate toward. The evil in our hearts cause the sin present in our civilizations.

Saint Augustine tells the story of Allipius, a student who went to Rome to study Law[72]. He was appalled by the gladiatorial games though they were the center of entertainment in Rome during his tenure. One day, a group of friends coaxed him into attending a game. He declared that while they may drag his body to the Colosseum, they could never make him watch or enjoy it. While sitting in the amphitheater and keeping his eyes closed, a scream from the arena filled the air and the crowd went crazy with excitement. He opened his eyes, he thought, to hate the spectacle all the more, but was drawn into the blood and instantly became so addicted to the violence in the games he withdrew from his school and laid waste to his professional life. The point is not watching a show will get us addicted, but rather, the sin in our world is so great we could be drawn into the evil with only a slight brush with sin.

This brush with sin is dangerous, and though watching wicked acts, particularly glorified sin, may not be sin itself, it would be foolhardy to think it does not impact our heart. Desensitization is the term for when we become susceptible to an attitude, concept, or even sin. The old story is of a frog in a pot. If the frog is placed in a pot of hot water, it will jump out immediately, but it is reported if the frog is placed in cool water and the heat gradually increased, it will eventually boil to death. Many pastors have said if we could freeze a devout Christian from the 1950's and thaw them out in modern days, they would believe the church has completely died while in their cryogenic sleep. Even our most perfect church couple would look destined to hell. Our culture has slipped into cold water long ago and failed to jump when the heat was readily applied. Through the humor, the constant programming, the small little offenses we let slide in the name of our entertainment, we have opened our eyes to greater sin and become cold to Christ's commands. We have forgotten our first love, and worse, we have paid Godless people our hard-earned money in exchange for pictures of sin desensitizing us to evil in our world. It is no wonder the church looks an awful lot like the world around us. But we can act and overcome evil. We can make ourselves sensitive again, we can turn back to the God who saved us.

As we consider media entertainment and become re-sensitized to the evil, we have to consider the reality of evil in the programming available today. Abstaining from entertainment is not always an option, and while too much consumption of television, video games, and Internet can certainly pollute our Christian life, some understanding of our culture may be required to connect with people in our life and in the world. We need to consider all elements of a fabulous story will contain some degree of evil. In fact, traditional story telling requires an element of evil, because again, without evil there is no hero fighting for the cause of goodness. So what is left for us to consider is our attitude about what we watch and how we entertain ourselves. If our attitude is one where we pleasantly enjoy death and murder, we need to examine our heart, but just because death and murder or even immoral sex occurs in a film it does not mean that we must totally abstain. We need to examine both the media and our hearts.

Ultimately, it is common to blame Hollywood and game designers for producing such morally bankrupt media, but these industries only respond to what makes money. The reason they produce such filth is because we, as a country, buy it. After all, companies failing to turn a profit go out of business and product lines that do not sell get discontinued. It is not a chicken and egg question that asks what was here first, the filthy entertainment or the moral decay in our society. It is clear, our society which professed for so long to be Christian, gave a monetary platform for writers and producers to profit heavily on sex and murder for mere entertainment value of sex and murder. As a result, the moral decay began to fester like the yeast of the Pharisees Jesus warned us about. Our society became filthy because we, as professing Christians, bought into decay and God was not amused.

We need to figure out how to be Christians in a world full of evil and sin without creating tiny bubbles to seclude ourselves within a warped subdivision of Christendom. We must be holy as God is holy (*1 Peter 1:16*), but still live in a world where we need to relate to the people around us without being judgmental or harsh, but loving. Though we may know and understand the world, we still must find the strength to live for Jesus in holy ways. We must stand ready to give a reason for the hope that is within us (*1 Peter 3:15*). In the next section of this chapter, we will discuss the balancing act in light of our entertainment purposes.

ENTERTAINMENT IN BALANCE

STAYING BETWEEN LEGALISM AND ANTINOMIANISM

As we consider how to balance enjoying entertainment with God's calling to holiness, we need to ask what is the difference between being holy and falling into either extreme of legalism and antinomianism. When the heart and the mind both unite to speak into our spirit what is right, we will come to the answer distinguishing these two errors. If we truly enjoy programs full of immorally sexual material (as a literal reading of the Bible would define immoral material), we have reason to question our heart. If we look at such material and think that type of entertainment is inconsequential to us, we may have fallen into antinomianism because we think no amount of law has any application to us. On the contrary, to hide under a rock and totally abstain from interacting with the culture may well be a sign of legalism. To watch a show containing some immoral content may not be *entirely* bad, but to pay no concern to the media we are consuming may be a sign we are among those whom Jesus never knew (*Matthew 7:21-23*). Clearly, we ought to be concerned about this balance.

Focusing more closely on legalism, I would place the people thinking Guitar Hero is sin (of course one version contains the song Mr Crowely!) as legalistic, but the Christian version available from CBD is clearly the saintly version of the game. We need to worry about surrounding our life with 'Jesus Junk' in the hopes that all of the Bible verses on our little trinkets might actually save us from sin like a talisman or crucifix is supposed to ward off evil. As Christian parents, we don't need to worry about letting our kids play some video games, but we should keep an eye on the types of games they play. One avid gamer in our day was not allowed to play *Super Mario Brothers* because a crazy 'Christian' speaker said Mario was a warlock because of the whole mushrooms and fire flower thing. Such a restriction is ridiculous! I think at the heart, a practical definition of legalism could be attempting to sanitize the world. The major problem with subscribing to legalism, however, is Jesus did not come to make bad people good, He came to make dead people live. Let's not be so concerned about whether we will pollute ourselves with a game, movie, or program on a basis of some really shaky logic.

On the flip side of legalism, a Christian would not think it right to engage in pornographic material, whether it is a game, a movie, or anything else. To make this point, I once dropped off a kid at home where the parent, a professing Christian, was watching the other child play a popular video game where the character was actually running around attacking people with a sex toy. That is clearly not the type of game a Christian should play, nor should a believing parent allow it in their home. The connections there are not some shaky theory about warlocks, mushrooms, and fire flowers, but rather, it is a connection full of gratuitous sin of paramount proportions. Biblically condemning a game where the player capriciously kills people and commits violent crimes is certainly not a stretch for the sound Christian. The same would apply for television programs where it is clear the makers want to mock God. If we enjoy such things, we are dancing on the edge of antinomianism and we should repent and remove such programming from our life.

THE GUARDRAILS

One summer I took a drive with a friend down a several hundred mile stretch of route 1 in California. The view is spectacular as the road follows the Pacific along the whole coast. At some points we parked the car to see the long, jagged decent into the ocean below and we saw just how tragic a fall off the road would be. I am glad there were guardrails on this highway in the event of a mishap on the road. Those guardrails could easily prevent a car from plummeting off the cliff. Just as you can think of those railings as protection from the dangers below, the Scripture affords that same protection to the believer. As such, the Bible warns of the dangers of sexual temptations:

My son, give attention to my wisdom,
Incline your ear to my understanding;
That you may observe discretion
And your lips may reserve knowledge.
For the lips of an adulteress drip honey
And smoother than oil is her speech;
But in the end she is bitter as wormwood,
Sharp as a two-edged sword.
Her feet go down to death,
Her steps take hold of Sheol.
She does not ponder the path of life;
Her ways are unstable, she does not know it.
(Proverbs 5:1-6)

We are warned to abstain from sexual immorality because God knows the problems we encounter when we have sex out of control. He knows of the emotional conflict and how many teenagers have ruined their life by having sex during a heat of passion, thus Paul writes in *1 Corinthians 6:18 - Flee from sexual immorality (ESV)*. So the warnings in the Bible can be thought of as guardrails. The dangerous road has two sides and holiness is associated with two false extremes. To remember the two keys of balance, we will commit two sections of Scripture to memory. With these verses memorized, we are then able to evaluate how to handle various forms of media entertainment.

LAW AND PROFIT

All things are lawful, but not all things are profitable. All things are lawful, but I will not be mastered by any. Paul wrote these words a few times in *1 Corinthians (6:12, 10:23)*. It appears that he was answering a question from the believers in Corinth, but we do not know the exact question. However, we can gather he is talking about some form of inquiry about permissibility. Paul addresses here and in other places that idols are just wood and stone, and food sacrificed to an idol is nothing except for one who is weak in conscience. He is likely speaking here of the problems of the often restrictive views of Jewish laws particularly as they related to Gentiles. He is saying God has made all things clean and so we need not be concerned we will accidentally fall out of favor with God. Remember the context that God may smite you dead if you disobeyed seemingly inconsequential rules (*Leviticus 10:1-2*), the actual Jewish word for God's name was never spoken so as to not accidentally break the commandment about using His name in vain, and let's not forget about that freaky incident with Anias and Saphira in *Acts 5.*

Indeed, this verse was a very freeing verse. It said God is not a cosmic security guard waiting with a baton to whack us when we step a foot out of line. Presently, Paul gives permission to Christians to be able to sit Jew next to Gentile in their meetings. He was clarifying that except the matters of the conscience, meat sold at the temple market was not a sin to eat and other 'taboos' of the day were permissible. Paul was not alone in his experience. In *Acts 10:9-16*, which we discussed earlier in this chapter, Peter was given the very same message.

Paul counter-balanced the lawfulness with a brief discussion about mastery. Addiction is the word we have today that might well be better than 'mastered' in this section. For something to master you, it must follow the traits of addiction (we will discuss addiction in the next chapter), but suffice it for now to say that *anything that does not directly violate the scripture or your conscience is permissible so long as it does not control you.*

ABSTAIN FROM EVIL

E **xamine everything carefully. Hold fast to that which is good and abstain from every evil thing.** In *1 Thessalonians 5:21-22*, Paul tells us to examine everything carefully. This is the most critical aspect of our present discussion and if more believers would simply do this one thing, I dare say we could turn the world on its head for Jesus Christ. *Examine everything carefully.* That means when you are watching a video game character beat people up with a sex toy, you can look at the situation and the Bible and say to yourself that this game is pretty clearly violating some commands in Scripture. If it is good, hold fast, if it is not, let it go. As I labored to say before, in order to examine everything carefully, we have to ask what we are examining it against. The answer is the Bible. Jesus says when we judge, judge with a righteous judgment *(John 7:24)*. That means we need to have some understanding about what the Bible actually says, so we should have taken the task to read it, study it, and let it soak into our mind. We are not looking for specific verses, but conceptual understanding.

The New Testament is very clear in many places about what is considered righteous and what is not. We need to find those sections of scripture and compare the words of the Bible to the entertainment we partake in. If we are finding a lot of what the Bible defines as evil, we should abstain. That will not be easy since we often default to define our entertainment by what gives us joy and sin can be entertaining. Regardless, let's be obedient to scripture and examine everything carefully. For now, hold fast to that which is good, and abstain from every evil thing while we prepare to dive deeper into this concept in Chapter 8.

Commit these two verses to memory and use them as the first step toward evaluating media entertainment. Remember first anything not explicitly condemned in the Bible is permissible as a Christian, but I take that to extend to any form of engagement. In order words, watching a film about immoral sexuality may not be the same as committing the sin, but it is so deeply connected Jesus said in the Sermon on the Mount whoever has lusted after a woman in his heart is guilty of adultery. We should treat what we watch with the same degree of concern. But on the flip side, we still need to examine everything carefully. That which is not evil, we are free to engage in, particularly those things which are lovely, pure, and noble. But keeping these verses in mind will help us to stay on the narrow path.

CHAPTER QUESTIONS

1. Would you rather error on the side or legalism or antinomianism? Why?

2. List some common gray area decisions. How do you respond to them?

3. How many money do you assume you have spent on entertainment that glorifies sin?

7

BREAKING THE POWER OF SIN

For what I am doing, I do not understand; for I am not practicing what I would like to do, but I am doing the very thing I hate.
– Romans 7:15

As Christians, we all struggle with sin. Paul was an apostle born out of time, nonetheless, seeing Jesus Christ with his own eyes (*1 Corinthians 15:3-11*). He was formerly a great sinner, murderer, and persecutor of the church. His struggle with sin should encourage us as we, too, fight our battles. Why is it we can remove some sinful tendencies from our life but others we cannot? Does not God have the power to overcome deeply-rooted sin and remove it completely from our life? Why can we love God so much and still battle sin in our heart? Paul asks these questions himself during his discourse on the fight within us:

> *I find then the principle that evil is present in me, the one who wants to do good. For I joyfully concur with the law of God in the inner man, but I see a different law in the members of my body, waging war against the law of my mind and making me a prisoner of the law of sin which is in my members. Wretched man that I am! Who will set me free from the body of this death? Thanks be to God through Jesus Christ our Lord! So then, on the one hand I myself with my mind am serving the law of God, but on the other, with my flesh the law of sin (Romans 7:21-25).*

If Paul wrapped up the discussion on this point we would have a very dismal outlook on our own life, and sadly because our single-verse culture fails to connect context across chapter lines, we forget *Romans 8*:

> *For what the Law could not do, weak as it was through the flesh, God did: sending His own Son in the likeness of sinful flesh and as an offering for sin, He condemned sin in the flesh, so that the requirement of the Law might be fulfilled in us, who do not walk according to the flesh but according to the Spirit (Romans 8:3-4).*

This is very easy to say, and very hard to do, so let's take some time to dig deeper into the interplay between sin and following God's path. I will submit that sinful addictions, what the King James Version calls a 'besetting sin' are differentiated from other sins.

UNDERSTANDING SIN

In order to delve deeper into our understanding of sin, we need to raise the controversial question of gradations of sin. This topic always creates an interesting discussion usually resulting from a lack of understanding of a few key verses. We need to understand when we are talking about gradations of sin, we are not suggesting that some sin is just 'little' from the eternal perspective. We know clearly and directly that **all sin separates us from God** (*Romans 6:23*). No matter how great the sin or how small the sin, we cannot enter the presence of the Lord because of our sin. We also know our sin is covered by the sacrifice of Jesus Christ for those who have placed their trust in Him (*Romans 3:24-26*). No sin, large or small, should ever be trifled with.

Even though our sin is covered by the Blood of Christ, not all sin is the same. Before you cry out declaring such statements as heresy, let's look at the evidence the Scriptures present. The least convincing is the logical argument stemming from Old Testament laws. *Leviticus 20* covers a variety of laws, the penalty for breaking these laws varies from being cast out of society to being put to death. Even our own legal system is based on similar gradations. Many states allow a death penalty for a person convicted of murder, and various other crimes hold with them a variety of different penalties. This alone would be flimsy evidence, but the New Testament alone contains many more verses to consider. *Mark 3:28-29* says:

> Truly I say to you, all sins shall be forgiven the sons of men, and whatever blasphemies they utter; but whoever blasphemes against the Holy Spirit never has forgiveness, but is guilty of an eternal sin.

Here is one example of an eternal sin. What does this sin mean? No one is completely sure and I am not about to attempt to explain it, I just want to show such gradations of sin do appear in Scripture. We find another argument from John:

> If anyone sees his brother committing a sin not leading to death, he shall ask and God will for him give life to those who commit sin not leading to death. There is a sin leading to death; I do not say that he should make request for this. All unrighteousness is sin, and there is a sin not leading to death (1 John 5:16-17).

To complicate the matter further, we also know different people are held accountable in different measures. *James 3:1* says:

> Let not many of you become teachers, my brethren, knowing that as such we will incur a stricter judgment.

Later in the book he says:

> Therefore, to one who knows the right thing to do and does not do it, to him it is sin (James 4:17).

All of these taken together suggest there are degrees of sin, and those degrees vary from person to person. Behold, the eternal judge measures each person perfectly, and Jesus declares He is coming and will give to each man according to his deeds (*Revelation 22:12*).

I do not raise the question about degrees of sin for a fruitless argument, but rather, because it is very important when considering our offenses before God, overcoming sin, and battling addictions. Sins which are not necessarily addictive in nature generally fall into categories of personal roughness and are usually related to how we are raised. A person from a loving and caring home will likely be a loving person, but one whom is from a home demonstrating poor manners toward others will likely be more abrasive of a personality type. It is up to the abrasive person, in Christ, to change his ways to become more loving to the world because that is the command from Christ:

> A new commandment I give to you, that you love one another, even as I have loved you, that you also love one another. By this all men will know that you are My disciples, if you have love for one another (John 13:34-35).

Other sins can be categorized by wrong thinking, merely needing a change in our mindset. An example of this would best be defined by little things including downloading movies on file sharing programs for which you have not paid, such is a violation of the law we are commanded to keep (*1 Peter 2:13-14*), and is stealing from the people who make a living producing such materials (*Ephesians 4:28*). Related is the person that brings office supplies home from work for personal use. Even though it is only paper, it is not your paper, and we as Christians are called to a higher integrity. Other life adjustments can be found in *Ephesians 4* including instructions on anger, falsehoods, clean speaking, and such things.

Of these sins, some are pretty easy to deal with. Unless you suffer from kleptomania, it is relatively easy to stop bringing home office supplies or downloading files you did not pay for. And if such materials are in your possession, delete the files, return the supplies, or offer to pay for them. Just make things right with the world and do not look to make yourself the exception to God's commands.

Some sins are deeply ingrained in our habits and become progressively more difficult to manage. I come from a family of gossipers. When I hear something that looks like criticism on someone else, my ears perk up, and I feel like I want to participate. As a former non-believer who worked in restaurants, I fully participated in these evil deeds. I knew who did a good job and who did a bad job and my self-righteous heart was the 'standard' and my mouth spewed forth 'truth'. I was totally in the wrong, and when I read verses such as these:

> Let no unwholesome word proceed from your mouth, but only such a word as is good for edification according to the need of the moment, so that it will give grace to those who hear (Ephesians 4:29).

> A perverse man spreads strife, And a slanderer separates intimate friends (Proverbs 16:28).

> If anyone thinks himself to be religious, and yet does not bridle his tongue but deceives his own heart, this man's religion is worthless (James 1:26).

> Whoever secretly slanders his neighbor, him I will destroy; No one who has a haughty look and an arrogant heart will I endure (Psalm 101:5).

> At the same time they also learn to be idle, as they go around from house to house; and not merely idle, but also gossips and busybodies, talking about things not proper to mention (1 Timothy 5:13).

I decided to change my ways. If I encounter a situation where people are talking in a gossiping-type manner, on a strong day, I walk away. On a weak day, I listen. On a bad day I join in. For me, because of my upbringing, I do not fight it daily like one fights an addiction, but I do need to carry verses like those above in my head for when the temptation is placed before me.

Progressing further, some sins fall into the category of addictions. An addiction is when a person is totally compelled to participate in the act. If the action itself is not a sin, the addiction to the action is a sin because an addiction places the substance of the addict above God. Remember we are to have no other God's before Him (*Exodus 20:3*). Though much idolatry is a personal choice, addiction crosses the realm into which the addict is compelled beyond their control to engage in idolatry. That is why addiction itself is a sin, regardless of the substance of abuse.

FIGHTING SIN

We all sin, it is sadly our human nature in our father, Adam. Even though we have his nature in us, once we become Christians we are given a new nature capable of keeping check on our sin. As I write this statement, I am not, in any way, implying we can reach perfection on earth. We will never reach perfection able to cut every bit of sin out of our life, but lack of perfection is not a reason to raise a white flag of surrender to sin. In chapter four, we examined the Biblical evidence for the command we have to battle sin. Almost every apostolic letter in the New Testament gave specific commands to repent from sin. Jesus tells the woman caught in adultery to *'Go and sin no more (John 8:11)'*. John the Baptist preached a baptism of repentance (*Matthew 3:1-12*). To read the Bible and believe we should not work on our sins would be dishonest to the Scriptures. James Montgomery Boice writes:

The Bible is written by God in order to provoke a personal response in us. If we don't allow that to happen, we inevitably misuse the Bible (even in studying it) and misinterpret it[73].

It is all well that we are commanded to leave behind our life of sin, but how do we actually break sin's power in our life? The first and most important truth is for those of us in Christ, it is only in Christ our sin can be conquered (*Romans 5:18-21*). We are a new creature in Christ (*2 Corinthians 5:17*). So our first and most important step in conquering our sin, is to believe in Jesus as our Savior and Lord.

Once we are born in Christ, the true battle over sin begins in our life. In the Sermon on the Mount, Jesus brings the life of the Gentile to the realm of thought. He preaches it is not enough to abstain from murder and adultery, but that letting your mind dwell on these sins is akin to committing them (*Matthew 5:22,28*). He gives the treatment analogy to remove the opportunity to commit the sin:

> *If your right eye makes you stumble, tear it out and throw it from you; for it is better for you to lose one of the parts of your body, than for your whole body to be thrown into hell. If your right hand makes you stumble, cut it off and throw it from you; for it is better for you to lose one of the parts of your body, than for your whole body to go into hell (Matthew 5:29-30).*

Since our thoughts are the first line of defense in cutting out sin, it is also appropriate Paul instructs us to bring every thought captive to the obedience of Christ so we can measure everything against God's truth (*2 Corinthians 10:3-6*). Romans says *the mind set on the flesh is death, but the mind set on the Spirit is life and peace (Romans 8:6)*. Our thoughts are the key factor in the health of our mind. If we are able to cast out the sinful thoughts, we will be able to progress toward Jesus, and the result is a life which becomes more and more like Christ.

The entertainment we watch will determine the content of our mind. Leading us to the next principle in our battle with sin which is to renew our mind. Paul writes to:

> Be transformed by the renewing of your mind, so that you may prove what the will of God is, that which is good and acceptable and perfect (Romans 12:2).

Renewing our mind is different from the second principle, cutting out bad media, in that our second step above is about removing bad influences. This step is to begin to add good influences. Paul again repeats this message in another way in Philippians 4:8 when he instructs us to let our minds dwell on good and honorable things. Peter tells us that we should *long for the pure milk of the word, so that by it you may grow in respect to salvation (1 Peter 2:2).* Renewing our mind will begin the process of crowding out sin.

Renewing our mind is not going to be possible until we flush out the old garbage. As Proverbs says:

> He who digs a pit will fall into it, and he who rolls a stone, it will come back on him (Proverbs 26:27).

We cannot clean our hands or purify our hearts while we allow filthy entertainment to cloud our minds. If we allow ourselves to be constantly amused by the things of the world, we are betraying the God who saved us, mocking His salvation. James wrote:

> You adulteresses, do you not know that friendship with the world is hostility toward God? Therefore whoever wishes to be a friend of the world makes himself an enemy of God. Or do you think that the Scripture speaks to no purpose: "He jealously desires the Spirit which He has made to dwell in us" (James 4:4-5)?

We must cleanse our minds by removing filthy entertainment and adding in the Word of God.

Finally, our battle with sin brings us to act out the teachings that are implanted by the Word. James says to *receive the truth implanted which is able to save your souls (James 1:21).* The apostle then continues on telling us that we should not only receive the truth, but also to put it into practice in real ways, not artificially:

> But prove yourselves doers of the word, and not merely hearers who delude themselves. For if anyone is a hearer of the word and not a doer, he is like a man who looks at his natural face in a mirror; for once he has looked at himself and gone away, he has immediately forgotten what kind of person he was. But one who looks intently at the perfect law, the law of liberty, and abides by it, not having become a forgetful hearer but an effectual doer, this man will be blessed in what he does (James 1:22-25).

James is not the only apostle with a direct command to do what is Godly. We already mentioned the words from Paul in *Ephesians 4:17-19* and *5:6-10.* Peter writes:

> As obedient children, do not be conformed to the former lusts which were yours in your ignorance, but like the Holy One who called you, be holy yourselves also in all your behavior; because it is written, "YOU SHALL BE HOLY, FOR I AM HOLY." (1 Peter 1:14-16)

Holiness is the command. To be holy is to be set apart, Godly, full of the character God calls us to live out. Jesus said:

> Not everyone who says to Me, 'Lord, Lord,' will enter the kingdom of heaven, but he who does the will of My Father who is in heaven will enter (Matthew 7:21).

So we are to live holy and it is very difficult if not impossible to maintain holiness in our life if our minds are constantly bathed in the sins of the world through media entertainment. Let us follow the command of Paul and set our minds on things above.

All this taken together, the best place to fight sin in our life and increase our Christian sanctification is to bathe our minds in the Word and take the Bible literally and seriously. Pray to God for help in your sanctification and grow close to Christ through time with Him. Cast aside the ways including the entertainment which aligned with the flesh nature and dwell rather on truth.

ADDICTION AND MEDIA

Addiction is a strong term conjuring up visions of drug addicts and crime, dirty clothes, and serious problems. May we not be like the Pharisee who proclaimed thanks to God that he was not like one of these, but rather we should be humbled by the words of Nathan, the prophet: *You are the man!* That may seem a little too strong but I will urge you to examine the possibilities, for many more people are addicted to media entertainment than are aware such a problem exists, and saturation with media can have a negative impact on our walk with God.

Addiction is complicated. It is not merely doing some detestable act, but is rather a deep compulsion to engage in the craving to the point the subject of addiction overtakes the rest of the person's life. Many addicts start to plan their day around their addiction. They get angry and irritable if they cannot engage their craving. Other family members need to accommodate the dependence, and co-dependency reigns supreme. Co-dependency is when the addicted person actually becomes the addiction of the non-addicted person. The co-dependent will arrange their life around helping the addict actually remain an addict! If it is alcoholism, the co-dependent will purchase alcohol, clean up the vomit, and cover up the mess that the addict makes, all while believing they are helping the family member. But to help the alcoholic drink more alcohol is dangerous to everyone involved.

Addictions generally start very small, like yeast in the manufacturing of bread or live bacterial cultures in the production of yogurt. Jesus warns the disciples about the leaven of the Pharisees (*Luke 12:1-3*). This is how a little bit of leaven is about to spread through the whole loaf:

Do you not know that a little leaven leavens the whole lump of dough (1 Corinthians 5:6)?

In this reference, Paul is addressing the old and new life. His message to the Corinthians is to let the new life spread rather than the old ways of living. But also in his message he is warning that a little bit of evil also will spread in the church. This is how addictions start and fester in our personal lives.

We first seek a little escape from the stress of our life through television or a game or a movie, then we start to like the feeling we get so we decide we are stressed a few days later and repeat the process. It again feels good, but we didn't notice we have spent a little more time on the game, or watched one more episode of the television program because we needed a break. This is where the seed of the addiction begins to take root: **we start to need the game or program to have a good evening.**

The rapid pace and over stimulation in media entertainment has certainly led to a high rate of media addiction. Norman Herr, Professor of Science Education at the California State University, Northridge lists some interesting statistics including 49% of people say they watch too much television, televisions are turned on in the home an average of 6 hours and 45 minutes daily, 66% of people watch television while eating meals, children watch an average of 28 hours of television per week. These statistics start to look like addiction. In addition to these numbers, Charles O'Brian at the Addiction Treatment Center at the University of Pennsylvania, also the chairman of the DSM manual lists physiological disorders included 'Gaming Disorder' in the DSM-V for the first time, though at the time of this writing, it is still in the section reserved for items that still need more research. Kimberly Young, a psychologist at the Behavioral Health Services division of the Bradford Regional Medical Center has created a therapy program for Internet addiction. In the true nature of addictions, she defines Internet addiction by the consequences of the Internet use, not the actual hours spent online.

Social media itself is believed to be a major source of addictions. Facebook, being the most known of the social media sites, gathers the flak of the genre like McDonalds gathers the criticisms of the fast food industry as a whole. One site wrote a satirical (I hope) article about Facebook addiction including these among other signs that you may be addicted to the social media site: Checking your Facebook whenever possible, Reporting on Facebook, Mad rush to add more friends, and the most significant in determining an addiction: Compromising offline social life. One YouTuber said Facebook should be called an Anti-social Network for the negative impact it has on our life. Facebook addiction, though not medically accepted at this time, is serious enough to find several step-by-step sites to overcome the habit. In true twelve-step fashion, all of the guides I read start with recognizing you have a problem.

Internet addiction is defined by consequences of internet use, not the actual hours spent online.

Video gaming is another addiction gaining attention in the media. The website simply called Video Game Addiction[74] lists several signs and symptoms of gaming and Internet addictions. They have compiled a list of what makes games addicting and also another list of the most addictive games. The top of the list is *World of Warcraft* (or World of Warcrack as some call it). This specially resonates with me since I was related a story of the addictive power of the game shortly after its inception. A case manager I worked with at Big Brothers, Big Sisters told me the case of a young man who was so addicted to the game he went through serious withdrawal when circumstances prevented him from playing. He ended up attending AA meetings to help get off the game. *Halo* was also listed as an addictive game, though the website is old, I would add several of the first-person shooter games, the most popular at the time of this writing being split between *Black Ops* and *Battlefield* (in their respective current renditions). Curiously, the other two games the site mentioned are *Solitaire* and *Tetris*. Though these games are simple, you have a desire to play again and again to beat your score (*Tetris*) or finish the game (*Solitaire*).

The biggest problem with media is it is designed to be addictive. The producers of these materials study how to get people engaged again and again. In the first chapter I described the progression of television from when I was a kid until now. While in the past, the programs were very segmented making it easy to stop watching after one show, the network has found out if they start the next show during the closing credits of the current show without a commercial in between, they increase the chance of your staying for another episode. The typical movie has increased in length and been designed to attract something in everyone to the point where even in many children's movies, kissing scenes are even expected. Video games have a greater ability to be addictive due to the ease of programming addiction into the game. They are challenging, but not so challenging they are impossible, but the achievement of small goals is easy. In *Black Ops*, the player develops their character by gaining better guns, equipment, or skills by playing more online games and achieving more skills. The small goals make the game easier to come back to over and over, particularly when the player can do a short timed game over and over in order to improve their overall kill ratio. Many of the newer games have two modes: a win condition for private play, and a mode to play with your online community in short win/lose games that can be played over and over like in *Solitaire*. The high score was classically the best way to get players in: beat the high score thus engraving your name on the digital screen. Ultimately the reason modern video games are so much more addictive than the games of the past is the online components. According to Video Game Addiction, it is these online communities where the average American teenager feels like he fits in while other places in the world tend to make him feel excluded. Ultimately, it is acceptance in the gaming world that keeps the kids hooked and playing.

As if the general addictive nature of playing the games was not enough, another recent controversy has arisen in the world of video games: Loot Boxes. The arrival of mobile and Internet gaming has led to an increase in 'microtransactions' which are little in-game purchases to help improve your gaming experience. These make the highly addictive video game industry also highly profitable by adding what many have called a gambling component. You pay with real cash and get a box that could randomly contain little trinkets or powerups, but also may contain legendary weapons, special characters, or other devices helping the gamer win. By making these available as a microtransaction many argued the video game creates addicts and then gives them a way to pay the game developers even more, and sadly these are usually kids being drawn into addictions with real money into the video game industry. While this is a new phenomena, many legislators in the United States and around the world are looking into laws banning this practice.

In the battle for our heart with addictions, whether it be drugs or games, the first step is always acknowledging the problem. The top signs of any addiction are a sense of happiness while engaging the object which can no longer be met by any other activity. When we are not engaged in our addiction, we are thinking about it. The activity starts to take up more and more of our free time to the point where our whole life starts to revolve around the substance of addiction. When confronted by the fact that we may be addicted, we either lie that it is not a big deal, or else joke about it even though we know we may have a problem. Finally, sleep becomes harder as we either think about our desire, or worse, dream about it to the point our conscious and subconscious mind are saturated in the addiction[75]. The bottom line, if we become consumed with wanting screen time more than doing our work, we may be dealing with an addiction.

To conquer the addiction, the addict must conquer the thinking accompanying it. It is not just a matter of the person deciding to change. When it comes to our sanctification, the Holy Spirit works within us to affect the change, but it is a joint process where we must participate. If we pray to God we will become holy, but we surround ourselves with godless entertainment, it will be like praying to God to become thinner, but failing to stop eating junk food. For this reason, counseling may very well be required to change addictive thinking, and we are right to focus on overcoming addiction as a part of our sanctifying process.

The most powerful factor to overcoming addiction is in making a decision to overcome. Once the decision is made, your life can be adjusted to account for your addictions. Some people will say that overcoming an addiction is merely a matter of choosing, but others have great difficulties with the change. Crowding out the addiction with activity helps some people. Jesus uses this as an analogy to cleaning sin out of our life:

> *Now when the unclean spirit goes out of a man, it passes through waterless places seeking rest, and does not find it. Then it says, "I will return to my house from which I came"; and when it comes, it finds it unoccupied, swept, and put in order. Then it goes and takes along with it seven other spirits more wicked than itself, and they go in and live there; and the last state of that man becomes worse than the first. That is the way it will also be with this evil generation (Matthew 12:43-45).*

What would happen if the demon came back to find the house occupied by the Holy Spirit? I dare to suggest it would wander on somewhere else. Some advocates for dietary change will suggest that instead of cutting out our favorite foods, we should first add healthy foods. Then when we gather new, healthier options, it will be easy to cut back on the foods that are not healthy. For the addiction, this translates into spending time with people who participate in activities other than the media for which we are addicted. It may mean we need to make conscience decisions about how we spend our time and try to weed out the addiction.

In my experience, the best way to alleviate the pull of the addiction is with Scripture. Not the regular advice of memorizing a verse counteracting addiction, but mass exposure to the Word. John MacArthur delivered a sermon titled *God's Word and Your Spiritual Growth* where he stated sanctification is achieved by exposure to Scripture. I would wager addiction is a breakdown of our sanctification and mere exposure to the Word is the absolute best way to restore the lost purity.

The exposure I am talking about requires planning time in the Word, and finding ways to spread Scripture throughout the day. I have tried starting the day with 3, 5, or even 10 chapters, but things always got in the way. I tried the same at night, but I was frequently too tired. This plan calls for creativity and I found the answer I was looking for on a TED talk about microhabits[76]. A microhabit is when a small habit is attached to an existing event. In my case I took to the speaker's plan and after I use the facilities, I read a chapter in scripture. This sounds horribly silly, and you may laugh at it, but it also has allowed me to read tons of chapters throughout the whole day. In the period of time where I have experimented with this approach, I have observed a clear increase in my heart, attitude, and knowledge of the Bible. If this is too extreme, try setting an alarm or timer on your phone where once per hour you take 5 minutes to read one chapter. If you are awake for 16 hours and you are able to do this 80% of the time, you will still read about 12 chapters a day and you will not have dedicated any specific time to read! That is the type of exposure to the Word I am talking about.

With our decision set to break media addiction and focus on the Bible, the next thing to do is plan to avoid situations where we will be tempted by the addiction. Remember *James 1:14-15*:

Each one is tempted when he is carried away and enticed by his own lust. Then when lust has conceived, it gives birth to sin; and when sin is accomplished, it brings forth death.

At least as a temporary measure, we want to avoid places where we are tempted by the addiction. This is a period of strengthening where we will be learning how to be strong against the object that makes us weak. In our case, avoiding the media entertainment from which you may be addicted.

Looking at practical steps as it deals with our topic, if our addiction is video games, identify the trigger and type of games. It may very well be possible to play games lacking an addictive nature. Find shorter games, or ones with shorter missions and see if you can handle just one. Avoid the addictive nature of live action role playing if you struggle with addictions. I would also recommend a fast from video games all together since they rarely add more to our life than entertainment anyway. Fasting is also appropriate for a movie or television addiction. Internet addiction is a little more difficult to deal with since it is almost impossible to live our modern life without it. A few people have undertaken the task of experimenting with life devoid of the Internet, but with difficulty, and usually having to result to a proxy to do a few tasks for themselves like scheduling for courses or communicating via online forums. Even at most of our jobs we have unfettered access to the Internet, so other measures may be required. Such home measures would include placing a filter on the Internet and blocking sites which are not required for living, or at least those sites taking time as an addiction. Have a friend or spouse set up the passwords so you cannot get in there and tinker with settings. Only that person should make adjustments to the settings and blocked websites. If our addiction could happen at work, it is critical but very difficult to talk to our supervisor so he or she is aware of the problem. They may be able to make sure the computer administrators are able to block access to addictive sites like Facebook or anything else you are struggling with. Whatever it takes, battle the addiction.

During this time, counseling or deep self-reflection will help us to identify the reason behind your addiction. An addiction usually has a specific trigger, and identifying such a trigger is the first critical step to overcoming. Sometimes an addiction goes back to childhood problems, it could be unfulfilled dreams or broken relationships. The dependency could very well end by searching for something deeper to do with our life. Spend time reflecting with God and searching for the reason behind the problems. It is critical during this period of time to be in the Word and reflecting. Jesus says in *John 8:31-32*:

> *If you continue in My word, then you are truly disciples of Mine; and you will know the truth, and the truth will make you free.*

Learning the truth of our life, soul, and joy can truly help us overcome our addictions. Only when we understand our purpose, can we truly be free. Remember God has a purpose for our salvation here on the earth:

> *For we are His workmanship, created in Christ Jesus for good works, which God prepared beforehand so that we would walk in them (Ephesians 2:10).*

With our life purpose identified and God's Word on our heart, we need to begin arranging our life to start fulfilling our purpose. Such purpose may need schooling or research, it may need a change in hours or a relocation. Whatever the purpose is, we will never escape addictions without fulfilling the purpose God has for our lives. But when we have identified the purpose and arranged our life to fulfill it, the object of our addiction can be placed in front of our eyes and we will joyfully cast it aside. That is the power of God in our life!

CHAPTER QUESTIONS

1. Have you ever battled an addiction? How has it compared to sin?

2. What tiny sins are in your life that could use some reteaching?

3. How 'Holy' are your entertainment choices? Is there room for improvement?

4. Do you think you may have a media addiction? Are you in denial?

5. What are the best steps you can do to grow closer to God?

8

EXAMINE EVERYTHING CAREFULLY

Examine everything carefully, hold fast to that which is good, abstain from every evil thing.
– 1 Thessalonians 5:21-22

Television, movies, music, videos on the Internet; they surround us, constantly bombarding our eyes and ears seeking an audience. While the democratization of the world lends to the perpetual opportunity to watch anything, almost anywhere, we must consider, as Christians, if we are totally free to watch anything we desire. Are there limits to what we, as believers, should consume when it comes to entertainment? Should we just blindly listen to the music and movie evaluations of critics or Plugged In Online? These are just some of the questions we will evaluate at present. We have already demonstrated we are living in fast-paced times where we have virtually no escape from media entertainment. Even when we are not constantly stimulated by movies and music in our home, the grocery stores, doctors offices, cafes, buses – everywhere we go, music is always playing subtly in the background. Total escape is not possible, and it is not even desirable because we live in and interact with the world. We must not consider music as evil when it is not praising God, well at least not most of the time. But all that being said, we should not just be totally passive in what we watch or hear. We should examine everything carefully.

DUBIOUS RATINGS

C ensorship is a very touchy subject. No artist wants to be censored. Even in my first book, *Testing and Temptations*, I referred to my childhood as a "living hell" in my draft, but my publisher at the time wanted the word "hell" edited out even though I believed it to be a very fitting description for my younger years[77]. Likewise, artists, particularly those whom do not believe in God, do not want to have their music or their movies censored. I stand by the freedom and ability to write and produce what we want, so free speech abounds. But I also agree with the necessities of ratings for those people who want to protect their senses and the senses of their children. All that being said, however, I believe the ratings systems in this country miss the mark on the protections they offer. In order to usher in a better model for us as Christians we need to first understand the history of censorship and ratings.

CENSORSHIP IN EARLY FILM

S ome of the early laws of our country were prudish but with good cause. Gambling, sexuality, alcoholism can destroy a society and many 19th and 20th century American laws reflected these concerns. As such, gambling on sports was illegal in the United States except Nevada in the late 1800's, so that is the state where a great boxing match was chosen to be held. For the first time, however, thanks to the progresses in the Industrial Revolution, film was created and the great Corbett-Fitzsimmons Fight commenced in Carson City, NV in 1897. It became one of the most significant films in history. It was significant because it was considered the longest single film to be completed to date, and it was the first film ever recorded in the widescreen format. But most significantly to our discussion here, it was the film which first prompted censorship laws in the United States.

While most states had laws on the books banning prizefighting, there were no laws prohibiting prizefighting films from being displayed. Due to the concern over the content of the film, two federal bills were proposed to ban the exhibition of the fight but neither bill was ever brought to vote. Though the federal regulators were slow to act, the Maine legislation moved rather quickly and on March 20th, only three days after the fight, a law was passed prohibiting the exhibition of the famous fight – punishable by a $500 fine. This began a wave of state regulations resulting in six other states banning the exhibition of prizefighting films. The regulations stemming from the boxing match were an example of regulation due to a disdain for an activity, but later regulations started to arise out of general morality[78].

In 1907 the Chicago city council gave the police authority to decide what movies were displayed in the city by issuing permits. Unlike the Maine and following statutes, these were not on the grounds of prizefighting or related exhibitions, but were decided on moral grounds and the law permitted either the complete removal of the film or else censoring out parts that would not pass the approval. In 1908, New York City followed suit, shutting down many theaters citing fire codes and moral concerns. In response to the mayor of New York City enforcing film censorship, a group of producers and distributors created the National Review Board. The producers voluntarily subjected their films to the scrutiny of the board and made the required edits to achieve the seal of approval. They voluntarily accepted the recommendations to appease governmental censorship, and for a generation of film such a strategy worked.

The creation of this first censorship board prompted other states to create their own boards. Some states required a review of the local board before films were allowed exhibition, but this cost extra money for the film industry. A nationally produced film would need to pay fees to several state boards in order to receive the seal of approval for showing movies, so in 1915 the Mutual Film Corp sued the Ohio Industrial Commission on free speech grounds, but the effort was a failure because courts determined for-profit business is not protected under free speech liberties of the constitution. The scattered laws and multi-state review board censorship remained in effect until the scandals of the 1920s.

The liberal, progressive lifestyle of the Hollywood players started to prompt concern in the people around the country. Still in effect was a general "company you keep" philosophy and many people including lawmakers were concerned Hollywood scandals would bleed over into the populous. Three high profile cases: Fatty Arbuckle was accused of (but acquitted in trial) rape and murder of Virginia Rappe; William Desmond Taylor was mysteriously murdered; Wallace Reid became addicted to drugs while recovering from an injury and eventually died in a sanitarium. These early high-profile cases once again threatened free speech in Hollywood and by 1921 several bills were introduced to protect the United States citizens from what was considered by some as riotous living. In order to once again counter the induction of bills into law, the Hollywood community created the Motion Pictures Producers, and Distributors of America (MPPDA) and appointed William Hays as the public relations officer. Within a decade, the Motion Picture Production Code (also known as the Hays Code) was in full implementation and adopted by all of the major studios. This was again to thwart government censorship by accepting voluntary input. The Production Code Administration enforced the code and the MPPDA agreed not to show any film that did not contain the PCA seal.

The Hays Code was restrictive, however. The movie industry agreed to accept the code to prevent financial losses while the economy recovered from The Great Depression. The acceptance of the code prevented controversy that empowered government legislators but it also kept the religious establishment happy – particularly significant because the church still held influence over their congregations – not to mention the code made the story making process easier. Very few twists were needed, the good guys and bad guys were clearly defined, and many action scenes were dictated, but not everyone agreed the Hays Code was good for the film industry.

Howard Hughes was the first major Hollywood player to challenge the production code. His monumental movie, *The Outlaw*, was rejected by the production code because the female lead had voluptuous breasts, though they were never exposed in the film. After many attempts to release the film and being resistant to the MPPDA, Hughes finally released the film under the United Artists label because they released films without the PCA seal of approval. Despite the controversy the film was a huge success and it demonstrated that even church-going populations were not fully on board with the Hays Code. The independent film associations began to grow in both the number of films released and in the money the production companies produced by selling the films. Eventually the popular films *The Moon is Blue* and *The Man With the Golden Arm* refused PCA censorship also becoming cash cows. Within five years of these films release, the production code crumbled as a rating system was established. While the code was restrictive as to what a movie could display, the ratings just informed the population as to the content of the material, but did not dictate what was in the film.

> Even church-going populations were not fully on board with the Hays Code.

Jack Valenti became the president of the Motion Picture Association of America while the production code was eroding. He proposed the ratings system which started with G M R X before evolving into the rating system we have now. The controversial part about the ratings now is the assignment of movie ratings has an arbitrariness. In the recent years, however, the ratings contain more information about why a movie has a particular rating, but there is no comprehensive public rubric exactly dictating what rating a movie will have (except we know a film can have one F-bomb before it rates higher than PG-13 – but even this is subject to change and is probably different by the time you are reading this).

Even though the code has evolved into ratings, it is the voluntary ratings system allowing us to be at an intersection between free speech and informed consent. While some have still protested and attempted to change what Hollywood does, we all have the opportunity to evaluate whether the content of a film is appropriate for us. The question for us as Christians is whether or not we accept the responsibility to evaluate the media at all.

ZAPPA, GORE, AND MUSIC CENSORSHIP

Not long after the movie rating system became mainstream, similar concern erupted over lyrical content in music. In 1985 opposing lines were drawn between Tipper Gore and Frank Zappa at the 99th Congress regarding the progression of sexually explicit and violent lyrics, mostly centered around heavy metal music. Parents and psychologists generally agreed with Gore that violent lyrics could impact the young listeners. Gore did not approach explicit lyrics with an eye toward banning or censorship as some have charged, but rather sought a voluntary rating system similar to that employed by the movie industry. She also wanted to see song lyrics made available to parents so they could analyze them prior to deciding whether a music album was suitable for their children. In all, Gore wanted ratings and lyrics available for parents to make informed consent regarding music choices for their children.

The entertainment industry obviously sided with Zappa in wanting to curb any form of regulation, voluntary or otherwise. However, many witnesses to the hearings, even some in the entertainment industry, had a problem with some popular heavy metal songs at the time. Judas Priest was only one artist whom had controversial lyrics. This is the tame verse in the song *Eat Me Alive*[79]:

> Sounds like an animal
> Panting to the beat
> Groan in the pleasure zone
> Gasping from the heat
>
> Gut-wrenching frenzy
> That deranges every joint
> I'm gonna force you at gun point
> To eat me alive

Due to concern over sexual activity elevated to rape and with a knowledge progression of musical content was getting worse, not better, eventually compromise was reached when the larger players in the entertainment industry agreed with Stanley Gortikov that adult-themed music albums should bear the now familiar Parental Guidance – Explicit Lyrics mark. At least we have that, though like many movie ratings, many parents just did not pay much attention.

The labeling was not followed by all producers in the music industry, however, and in 1990 a music album was deemed in one state to be obscene, and store owners were arrested if they were caught selling the album. 2 Live Crew were noted for being an overly obscene band and they released their album, *As Nasty As They Wanna Be*. Even the song titles are too obscene to list here, let alone the lyrical content. During the fallout of the album controversy, three band members were arrested for performing their songs, but the members were acquitted and the obscenity label on the album was eventually overturned on free speech grounds. This is just one example of lyrics out of control.

Of course in our modern day, we can now find all of the lyrics to an album prior to purchasing, but we still do not have anything in the music industry that resembles the voluntary ratings system found in the other major media forms.

EASIER ROAD TO TELEVISION RATINGS

While the movie rating systems came after many long battles and court cases, the proliferation of television in the late 1980s and early 1990s prompted a discussion about the content on TV. As a child we never saw any ratings preceding television programs. Most television was tame enough to not merit obscene content at least during hours when typical young people were awake, and most of society generally agreed on what content was appropriate and networks displayed clean content at least until 11:00 PM. Of course, George Carlin performed his famous *7 Words You Can Never Say on Television* routine in 1978 which marked the beginning of the end for decent open-air television[80]. Some content like *The Simpsons* started to push the envelope when it was released, but critics of the popular *South Park* said that show did not just push the envelope, it knocked it off the table! *South Park* was released the same year the ratings became mainstream for broadcast television.

The television rating system was first discussed by Republican Senator Paul Simon who became concerned with the increase in objectionable content over cable and broadcast TV. The discussions with networks first occurred in 1994, then guidelines were proposed in 1996, and by January 1997 the FCC and congress implemented the guidelines as voluntary ratings to be placed on programs. The broadcast companies knew from the history of ratings in Hollywood that voluntary participation is always better than fighting the government, and ratings are better than censorship because the producers can still do what they want; they just need to alert the people to the content via the ratings. This was combined with a law requiring chips be built into any televisions made after 2000 that allowed content to be blocked on the television set based on ratings. This was a good compromise in the opinion of the networks, and I agree. With these guidelines in place, studios can create what they want and I can limit the viewing in my home, but we need to be intentional in our personal viewing habits.

VIDEO GAME RATINGS

The timing and process of video game rating mirrors that of television programming, but regulation is actually older than both television and music censorship. In 1976 the first graphically controversial video game, *Death Race*, was manufactured. In the game, players amass points running over 'gremlins' that were obviously crudely drawn. The game had a working title of *Pedestrian* and it is clear that the game was truly about running over people because it was based on the controversial dystopian movie *Death Race 2000* depicting a government paying people in an annual race to kill off extra pedestrians in a national cross-country race. Though this game did not experience massive sales (only 500 copies were manufactured), it did show that some sectors of society were interested in such video games.

As the Atari 2600 gained market popularity, a pornography company set up a video game division called Mystique and manufactured a number of pornographic video games for the Atari. These games included *Custer's Revenge* where the player was a nude male seeking to rape native American women. *Beat 'em and Eat 'em* was an Atari game about masturbation. Atari 2600 sued the game manufacturer to stop the production, but leaving the Atari system open wide for third-party game manufacturing prevented any possibility of controlling the content played on the console.

In 1983 Atari encountered setbacks due to low quality games which eventually led to the video game crash. The setbacks mostly occurred because Atari placed excess financial resources into the rushed *E.T.* video game which ended up being one of the worst Atari games ever[i]. The company never recovered, but Nintendo was gearing up to refresh the video game market with the 1985 Nintendo Entertainment System (NES) in the United States market. Being privy to the pornographic video games that plagued the Atari and not wanting the negative backlash, NES featured a lockout chip that prevented unlicensed games from running on the system. This created an opportunity for Nintendo to better regulate the video games that would play on their console, and they had a family-friendly business philosophy excluding gore, sexuality, religious expressions, and other topics taboo to the mid 1980's culture. While Nintendo maintained video game market dominance, the gaming industry was not a

---

[i] The Extra Terrestrial video game was so bad they were pulled from the market and the excess copies were buried in a New Mexico landfill only to be recovered several decades later. After such a resurrection the game has become a huge collectors item.

concern to parents, religious groups, or government agencies, up to this point.

Sega was gearing up to release the Genesis console featuring better graphics than the 8-bit NES system. Though Nintendo was also preparing for the Super Nintendo as a graphically competing console, Sega remembered that controversy sells. During the release of these systems, *Mortal Kombat* was a very popular arcade game. (I remember playing it in the local bowling alley which probably made more money on that game than on bowling any given night!) Because of the game popularity, the developers wanted to port the game to the two competing consoles, but Nintendo cut out the gory kill moves in keeping with their family friendly philosophy. Sega allowed the gore which helped the sales. When *Mortal Kombat II* was set for release, Nintendo finally allowed the full gore version on their console, but Sega had already won the match with this game. The decision did make for better sales, but at the cost of raising awareness to progressive violence and gore in video games, as was happening in the television, movie, and music industries.

Like the movie and television industries, the gaming industry was coming to the conclusion it needed to either check its own conduct or else face government regulation. This led to the industry coming together like the television producers to produce a voluntary video game rating system. Though the rating system is voluntary, many major retailers choose not to sell games that do not participate in the ratings system. However, the ever-changing media culture has pushed back and Steam, one of the largest and most influential single game purveyors of our age has just allowed (in 2018) the first ever unedited, full-frontal adult-themed video game[i]. *Negligee: Love Stories* is a novel-type story

---

[i]Steam is owned by Valve and they do not create the video games. They are merely a platform for game creators of any kind to list their video games for sale.

based video game featuring nudity, sexual content, and dialog. It will not show up in searches unless the user specifically sets their account to look for adult themed content...for now. But with this game penetrating the market, it is only a matter of time before the floodgates are opened and such games will be widely available and sexual-themed games will become all the more common.

So we see that the entertainment industry in most forms does regulate itself, though mostly to avoid governmental scrutiny. And such regulation is more open to the subjective whims of the audience as those who care about the media entertainment in our culture grow smaller in number. With such regulation at hand, why are we even considering our own evaluation? Why not just accept what the industry places as its ratings and choose based on those ratings what is appropriate? The ultimate answer to all these questions is the purpose of this world is misaligned to God's purposes, so we will consider who should evaluate media entertainment for ourselves and why.

THE CHRISTIAN RESPONSE

As Christians, we should be concerned with the material we consume, but the culture's solution is inadequate for the standards and purposes of God's people, so we should seek the character of God to understand media entertainment. As we embark in our journey through media evaluation, we should consider our purposes and goals. Primarily, we must be obedient to God. He would rather we not sin to begin with as opposed to repenting of our sins. In *1 Samuel 15*, Saul is in an exchange with Samuel whom is bearing a frightful message from God. Saul thought the purpose of God was to offer sacrifices like the pagan nations around him, but God was more interested in obedience. Here is the conclusion to Samuel's remarks in *verses 22-23:*

Has the LORD as much delight in burnt offerings and sacrifices
As in obeying the voice of the LORD?
Behold, to obey is better than sacrifice,
And to heed than the fat of rams.
For rebellion is as the sin of divination,
And insubordination is as iniquity and idolatry.
Because you have rejected the word of the LORD,
He has also rejected you from being king.

Secondly, we are being obedient to God out of our love for our savior, not because we are focused on rules. *John* writes in *14:21:*

He who has My commandments and keeps them is the one who loves Me; and he who loves Me will be loved by My Father, and I will love him and will disclose Myself to him.

Though fear of God is the beginning of wisdom and the start of our obedience, it is the love we have for our God which ultimately drive us to obey.

Thirdly, we must consider if we are called to evaluate media for ourselves or if we can simply allow other people to inform us in their evaluations. In general, we should never take all of our information from one source. We as people can make mistakes and discernment is achieved by considering multiple points of view. We must take to heart the lessons from the Bereans in *Acts 17:11:*

Now these were more noble-minded than those in Thessalonica, for they received the word with great eagerness, examining the Scriptures daily to see whether these things were so.

With that in mind, if we are parents or mentors of kids, we should be far more vigilant of popular culture than people who rarely watch television or listen to music. It does not fall to all of us to analyze everything the culture produces because there are different parts of the Christian body and some may be better suited and have a heart to keep tabs on the culture for the rest of us. For those of us who find it necessary, I will provide the general guidance which has worked well for me over the years in the next chapter.

THE MESSAGE MATTERS

The first principle is concern over the message the producers are trying to teach. Just because vulgar language, sexual activity, or excessive violence appears in a film, it does not mean that I am never going to watch it, though caution is advised. For example, a movie probably rated NC-17 or higher was released in the early 2000's called *Kids*. The movie followed inner city teenagers as they lived their regular days getting drunk, dealing in drugs, gang-beating a person on the street, and engaging in sexual 'conquests'. Due to the graphic content pervasively throughout the movie, it is certainly not in my collection, however, the point the producers convey through the film is a powerful lesson in the consequences of unsupervised teenagers in the city streets[81]. If the movie finally glorified these actions as in the popular *American Pie*, where the cast is celebrating the loss of their virginity, I would simply call the film filth, but in *Kids*, the main co-star, Telly, is revealed to have contracted AIDS and his counterpart, Casper, finally rapes the girl who discovers she has contracted AIDS from Telly. The movie ends in the classic scene of a hung-over and naked Casper slurring the final line in the movie: "what happened?" The point is clear: drugs, out of control sex, and unsupervised teenagers in the city streets is not good for any culture. They paint a horrible picture of the party scene far from the glorified view depicted in *American Pie*. The purpose and the message of the film is highly important as the message penetrates our heads whether we think about it or not.

When considering the message a film, game, or artist tries to make, we will reach back into the earlier chapters and use our knowledge of the Bible as our guide. The Bible does teach homosexuality is a sin, and while I cannot ask non-believers to adhere to such belief, God is clear in restricting Christians from engaging in homosexual behavior (just like we should not engage in fornication or adultery). On such basis, films such as the *Crying Game* which are produced to teach us sexual love knows no gender are not the types of film which are appropriate for a Christian to use for entertainment[82].

Ultimately every television program and movie, every song, and most albums seek to teach us something. The question becomes, will we let their messages tinker around in our head without evaluation or are we better off to think about what the producer is trying say? *Family Guy* is a popular television program seeking to mock religious faith and cultural taboos, though I know several professing Christians who like to watch the program. The producers seek to break down all sins, and it would appear that they made an attempt to fit a violation of everything that the Bible holds sacred into their series. The program mocks God and seeks to further stereotypes of incompetent men, near perfect wives, kids that get away with everything, and more. Back when *The Simpsons* premiered, the program was heralded as controversial, but now it is one of the most tame cartoons on television; a time capsule to the shifting landscape of media entertainment. Other notable programs with a horrible message include the new television series, *Lucifer*, where the protagonist (you know, the guy we root for) is actually the Devil. When I first saw *Lucifer* advertised, I knew I wanted to evaluate a few

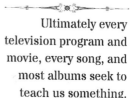

Ultimately every television program and movie, every song, and most albums seek to teach us something.

episodes. I actually forgot about the program until an older church woman talked about how much she liked the show. I quickly watched a few episodes online and was promptly worried. In this show, Lucifer certainly is carnal. He owns a night club (with a succubus as his bar tender), engages in all sorts of pleasurable sin, but is deeply disturbed in the death of people. He frequently refers to his 'Father' (of note – we are made in God's image, the angels are not; they do not refer to God as the Father like we do), but of a stained love and he is always seeking reconciliation with his father. Also of note, as he does 'good deeds' in one episode, he starts to feel closer with his father. This is clearly confusing theology, fanciful, and in my opinion, dangerous.

Also on the topic of horrible messages, I would place several supposedly Bible-based movies such as *Noah*, *Exodus*, and *The Bible* television series which first debuted in 2013. I elevate these to the potential danger list because the stories often veer off the path of Biblical accuracy in places the scriptural text is clear. Obviously I do not have a problem with well placed filler material like that we saw in several scenes in *Risen*, but the *Exodus* movie was so far from the Biblical account of the actual story that I was waiting for Batman to rise and save Memphis from the evil Pharaoh. How they could get the name of Moses son, Gershom, correct, but leave out the fact that Moses's staff was the object of the miracles is beyond me. In the movie, Moses gives his shepherds staff to Gershom and takes his sword back to lead a warring rebellion against the Egyptians, and that is not the worst part of the film[83]. The reason I take such offense at the production is because, as George Lucas observed, film plays a larger role in our modern-day life than the Bible or church events, and it will become easier to watch these accounts rather than reading the true history in the Bible. This results in a shift taking less than one generation for errors portrayed in the movies to become cemented as 'common knowledge' of what the Bible really teaches! We do not want to come to a point where Josiah found himself when he believed he was following God until the priests found the dusty old Bible long since forgotten. We, too, are becoming a 'Christian' people who believe we are following and serving God even though the Word of God is far from our hearts. The message matters, my friends.

GLORIFICATION OF SEXUAL SIN

The second principle I use in evaluating media is to examine the sexual content and purposes. One observation indicated that if a couple were married in the course of the film, it often marks the end of romance. The best sexual encounter according to Hollywood is either fornication or adultery; anything else is just boring. The reason I pull sexual sin from the other sins in my list is because Paul also made a differential distinction in *1 Corinthians 6:18*:

> Flee immorality. Every other sin that a man commits is outside the body, but the immoral man sins against his own body.

That being said, sexual content present in film is not reason enough for an adult to avoid a film or television program, but if such a sin is glorified, it marks an occasion to erode our conscience. Remember James says:

> Each one is tempted when he is carried away and enticed by his own lust. Then when lust has conceived, it gives birth to sin; and when sin is accomplished it brings forth death (James 1:14-15).

Avoid the glorification and you will avoid a lot of pressure to engage in sexual sin.

To understand the difference between glorification of sexual sin and its mere presence, I will consider three factors. The first consideration is if the production callously uses sex as a plot line devoid of warnings. One of the most popular films in 1999 was *American Pie*. The entire film followed a group of high school friends with a goal to lose their virginity by prom night. The morally bankrupt story follows their exploitative attempts and final victory where the credits role to satisfaction of their conquests accomplished. The pregnancies, sexually transmitted diseases, and moral regrets are all absent from the story line which focused only on having sex at any cost[84]. Another film surfaced a few years later, *Anchorman*, which was so vile I had to leave the room when my companions decided to watch the movie. Of course our more recent years have seen the sensationalism of the *50 Shades of Grey* series, which is nothing more than soft pornography, unfortunately viewed by Christians and non-believers alike. The *50 Shades of Grey* franchise alone has generated $1.2 billion dollars of profit as of only 2017. Like the films which surfaced to annihilate the Production Code, these film franchises have amassed a combined billions of dollars becoming raging successes, and the immoral sexuality was key to their success in each case.

In more recent decades, television programs, movies, music, and even video games have started to glorify immoral sexual activity. In *Lucifer*, the Devil is into immoral sex, and this is the character we are to make a connection toward through his story[85]. Even the cartoon genres including *Family Guy* are interested in breaking every sexual taboo from pornography to bestiality[86]. Video games cannot escape sex due to one of the most popular video games on the market depicts game segments where the hero engages a prostitute. Not to mention to the subsequent release of sex-focused independent games which are now available on Steam, a gaming repository used by many American youth. Sex is out of control in our modern entertainment and the more of that content we buy, the more of it the producers will create. The Christians must take a solid stand against these types of entertainment, not just in pickets or public outrage, but by silently obeying God and not putting filth before our eyes. Only when we choose not to spend our money on filth collectively will production companies get the picture we do not need sex in every form of entertainment for which we engage.

My second consideration is whether the character learns over the course of the program. The movie *Playing for Keeps* has our hero falling into sexual contact mostly due to a lack of established boundaries, but by the end of the film he is starting to mature and attempts to regain the trust of his son and former lover. While we see him engage two women that seduced him, we also see the character resist two other women by the end of the film[87]. Though this is not as pure as it could be, we do see the dynamic character learn a lesson by the end of the show and this is commendable. Sexuality is an important part of the human psyche and it cannot be ignored completely, so if a character learns not to engage in this risky activity outside appropriate boundaries by the end of the film I can support the encounters as part of the learning process.

Third, sexuality can be used as a means of a lesson by showing us the consequences of sin. We talked about the 1995 movie *Kids* earlier. To recap, the story follows some inner city teenagers as they engage in sex, drugs, gang fights, and parties. One of the girls, Jennie, has only had one sexual encounter which was with the main character, Telly, who is portrayed as engaging in many sexual conquests. Jennie receives the results of an HIV test and it proves positive for the disease. She seeks out Telly to find he has already left the party to go off with another young woman, but Telly's best friend, Casper, rapes her in the night. The closing scene in the movie is Casper sitting naked on the couch with the always-uttered after party phrase: What happened? The point of the film is clear: Casper, in your drunken stupor you raped a girl with AIDS! This is an extreme case, but it well exemplifies that sex can be used to teach us the physical consequences of sexuality outside marriage and commitment. More appropriate and practical examples might include the movie *Simon Birch* where Joseph is born a bastard child and his mother had never revealed the identity of his father. The touching movie takes a turn when his mother dies while Joseph is 12 years old and he is stuck in an identity crisis between a dead mother and an unknown father[88]. The point can be extracted that immoral sexuality created a child who had to work through his issues at a young age. Of course, this movie only mentions the encounter, but does not contain any sexual scenes which makes it a much better case to teach this lesson than the former example.

The mere presence of sexual themes should not deter mature adults from a film in itself, but be aware sex as mere humor in places the Bible would call sinful may erode our ability to resist the Devil in sexual temptations. If the sexual themes are to teach us a moral lesson drawing us closer to God through teaching us consequences than sexual themes may not be a final deterrent to watch the film.

REBELLION AS THE HERO'S WAY

The third principle is more general than the previous two. I want to know what is the total disposition of the hero toward rebellion. If the protagonist revels in rebellion causing us to cheer for him to do what is wrong, the program will likely lead us down a rebellious path. *1 Samuel 15:23* quoted in context above says:

For rebellion is as the sin of divination,
And insubordination is as iniquity and idolatry

While the abundant sin in *Natural Born Killers* was murder, the story line as reported by the characters was more about rebellion than anything else. The subjects of the movie were two mass murderers on a killing spree across the country for no particular reason. They are eventually caught and imprisoned but they escape after starting a riot by becoming a media sensation by declaring in a prison interview, "I'm a Natural Born Killer". The film ends by killing the interviewer who was creating a video exposé of the couple. The film was a timely mirror of our violence-obsessed culture and how we glorify mass killers, but by making the film in the eyes of the perpetrators they effectively glorified the killings adding gasoline to the fire of violence. Notice here the intention of the film is not my concern, it is the glorification of the sin. Since this movie left off with the closing scene of killing the final victim while the protagonists walked off gleefully smiling, the producers clearly sent a message that violence is enjoyable.

From the same era, *Fight Club* followed two characters who were really one in the surprise final twist. The main character, Tyler Durden and alter-ego 'Jack', are a one-man criminal master mind team who engages in general chaos and rebellion through a program called "Project Mayhem". They killed several people, particularly wealthy or powerful people whom the general population may feel a disconnect toward. They blew up buildings and all because the main protagonist was frustrated with the daily grind of life. It was the ultimate film in 'going postal' taking vengeance on the world around us. Ultimately, the rebellion against the ways of the world in this case led to much greater sins[89].

Eric Holmberg, founder and president of *Reel to Real Ministries*, observed that if you can get a person to rebel, you open up a wide array of sins. Rebellion lends itself to out of control sex and killing that we have already discussed. Rebellion in the course of a production can take the form of bullying, vandalism, drunkenness, and other sins Paul recorded in *Galatians 5:19-21*:

> *Now the deeds of the flesh are evident, which are: immorality, impurity, sensuality, idolatry, sorcery, enmities, strife, jealousy, outbursts of anger, disputes, dissensions, factions, envying, drunkenness, carousing, and things like these, of which I forewarn you, just as I have forewarned you, that those who practice such things will not inherit the kingdom of God.*

When the protagonist glorifies and revels in these sins, we start to feel accustomed to the sins in our daily life. In a time when our influence through church programs and Christian study is on steady decline and media entertainment rapidly increases, it is not entirely unexpected we would see a large outpouring of violence in our world. What may start as a little seed of rebellion may end with shipwrecking our lives upon our own decadence. The apostle Paul writes, *Bad company corrupts good morals* (*1 Corinthians 15:33*), and we are generally spending more time with Hollywood productions than we are with Godly endeavors.

THOSE UNSETTLING FILMS

In recent years some films have appeared containing interesting and unsettling messages and meanings. These films demonstrate a degree of violence, but also certainly contain some fascinating themes. In the movie *Devil*, five people are trapped in an elevator under suspicious circumstances. The people are getting killed one by one as rescue workers try to get into the elevator. It turns out the people are dying for their sins. The plot twist is the Devil is in the elevator killing them, but he is not able to kill the final person because he confesses his sin. The man's sin is that he killed a woman and child in a hit and run accident five years earlier but was never caught. When he confesses his crime, the police detective makes the arrest and we clued in that it was the detective's wife and child. Rather than being hateful toward the killer, he realizes the five years taught him about forgiveness, which was the final theme of the film[90]. You can see this is not Biblical forgiveness or the way the Devil operates, but it is still an interesting movie about how providence can balance good and evil.

Another unsettling film is *The Book of Eli*. In this post-apocalyptic world, the main antagonist is searching the remaining world for a special book he remembers from the old world which has the power to control people. He has roaming marauders searching everywhere for the book and then suspects the hero of the movie, Eli, posses it. Eli has been following God as he is led west. We encounter fighting, vulgarity, drunkenness, and some sexual sins over the course of the movie. We also learn Eli is traveling for about thirty years, even though he could have made it west in much less time. The villain does finally acquire the book through violence and we learn three amazing facts. First, Eli is actually blind, but he can read the book which is written in Braille. Second, God had him wandering so long because Eli was memorizing the whole book, and finally, the book is the Bible, and Eli the chosen instrument to bring it to Alcatraz where a collection of old world artifacts was to help civilize the new world[91]. Given the content, this is not a movie for the younger audience, but the final message is quite fascinating, also given that the antagonist's back story included a mother who was overly engaged in watching televangelists who could control the people, acquire wealth from the audience, and leave them wondering what this God really ever did. Fascinating movie indeed.

The Passion of the Christ would also appear in this list of films. Though it was horribly violent, many families took their younger children to watch it because of the message of Jesus[92]. The authenticity of the film became a selling point since they chose to film it in the ancient Greek language. The imagery present in the film was mostly faithful to the Bible story, but the criticisms came from the excess amount of blood in the flogging scene. Still, many of the more astute, violence-conscious parents let their kids watch the film because it was specifically about the final days of Jesus and His ultimate sacrifice.

Taken together, these movies illustrate the point I am making in that the message is more important than the content. Each of these films portrayed violence and sins, yet each one ended in a powerful message. The sins were not glorified, rebellion is not celebrated, and the meaning rang true for those who were looking for it: God is in charge of the world, and forgiveness is available for the taking. If we let black and white rules for quantity of blood, the presence of sexuality, or the use of vulgar language dictate our decisions, we may be setting up our families, our faith, and our world for a utopic fantasy devoid of reality.

Peddling R Rated Reading Material

These final movies grant us challenges to black and white censorship. Adopting such dichotomy, what would you think of a book describing love relationships between two people written in graphic words for the time period it was written? What about a book that describes murder, pride, jealousy, war, theft, and all sorts of sins. How do we respond when our pastor tells us to read the Bible? The Holy Bible is full of objectionable material. The pages exude blood, sex, violence, and the like. It speaks to general observations about righteous men frequently being persecuted while the wicked prosper (*Psalm 73:3, Jeremiah 12:1*). If we just throw away every production containing objectionable material we might as well just throw out our Bible...but we instead encourage people to read it. We are pleased to see our kids read the pages of the scripture and almost every program for the youth requires the kids to even memorize verses (albeit not the violent ones), but the point remains. If the Bible is taken as a collective good because of its core message, we should consider media with a similar approach. Obviously the Bible is the inspired word of God and media is not, but we are all made in His image and as such, many important truths can be found all around us. As one person said, intelligence is learning from your mistakes but wisdom is learning from the mistakes of others. We can acquire wisdom from media, but we also must balance this with the words of John MacArthur: When human wisdom is right it agrees with the Bible so we don't need it, but when it is wrong it is against the Bible so we don't want it[93]! Media should be approached in the same manner.

Ultimately, we should indeed limit our media entertainment and always make sure the written Word of God is the center of our life, but when we do consume Hollywood productions we need to evaluate the material and the message so we are not pulled into the sin of the world on the one hand but we are not so separate from the world as to be unrelatable on the other. Our mission is still to reach the people in our life where we are for Christ. Put down the remote and keep true to our calling to reach our world for Christ.

CHAPTER QUESTIONS

1. How do you use movie ratings in your own entertainment? Do you find ratings sufficient?

2. Is industry regulation better or worse than government regulation?

3. Think of the popular expression, "It is better to ask forgiveness than permission". How does *1 Samuel 15:22-23* reject such a notion?

4. Using the methods of media evaluation herein, what plan can you create to evaluate media entertainment?

5. Have you ever considered violence in the Bible and how it is similar to media entertainment?

9

OUR FINAL RESPONSE

For we are His workmanship, created in Christ Jesus for good works, which God prepared beforehand so that we would walk in them.
- Ephesians 2:10

A CALL TO UNDERSTAND

W hy should we even consider media? Very simply because media is the primary language used by the unsaved world we are called to reach. Stuart McAllister observed media has so infiltrated our culture it permeates everything we think, speak, and do. At its core, our western society is addicted to modern media, and we speak the language of popular arts in terms of what is presently popular on television, Netflix, and YouTube. Some dive too far into this manufactured reality making the church itself an extension of the media, and embrace with open arms popular culture's infiltration into the church. On the other hand, some churches want absolutely nothing to do with media in the present form, denouncing it all as the Devil's work. Both of these approaches have their valid concerns, but also present problems.

For the churches who embrace the culture, those cultural mores creep into the church and influence the leadership and congregation more than the Scriptures. As people, we are easily entertained and seek the path of least resistance. After all, the great C.S. Lewis said:

Indeed the safest road to Hell is the gradual one--the gentle slope, soft underfoot, without sudden turnings, without milestones, without signposts[94].

We naturally seek what is easier and what feels better, and meaning entertainment becomes our orthodoxy, as I explained in chapter 5. When churches start heavily promoting popular media, it becomes a distraction from the Bible, the things of God, and service. The congregation morphs into worldly disciples, loses sanctification, and fails to seriously evaluate the popular arts. They have forgotten *1 Thessalonians 5:21-22*:

> *Examine everything carefully, hold fast to that which is good, abstain from every evil thing.*

On the other hand, churches wanting to remove all references to media on the basis of being part of the Devil in the Devil's world are forgetting that even the apostle Paul used the secular arts of his day to preach:

> *For in Him we live and move and exist, as even some of your own poets have said, 'For we also are His children.' (Acts 17:28)*

When the church pulls completely out of the world, including the media, the members become out of touch with the world they are called to reach with the Great Commission. Once they lose touch they become what some have called, so spiritually minded they are no earthly good. Once this happens there is no framework left to talk to people about the human condition, the pains and problems life present, but since they do not speak the language of the media, they find themselves trying to talk to people in foreign dialects failing to meet them in the common ground of communication.

The result of the first church in our discussion is a congregation with nothing to offer the world. They have fallen into the very world system for which they are tasked with separating themselves from and simply trying to add Jesus as a capstone to purify their choices. They fail because the church is called to be holy, separate:

> Do not love the world nor the things in the world. If anyone loves the world, the love of the Father is not in him. For all that is in the world, the lust of the flesh and the lust of the eyes and the boastful pride of life, is not from the Father, but is from the world. The world is passing away, and also its lusts; but the one who does the will of God lives forever (1 John 2:15-17).

So while we are called to be separate, if we have no connection to the world, we have no starting point of relationship:

> For though I am free from all men, I have made myself a slave to all, so that I may win more. To the Jews I became as a Jew, so that I might win Jews; to those who are under the Law, as under the Law though not being myself under the Law, so that I might win those who are under the Law; to those who are without law, as without law, though not being without the law of God but under the law of Christ, so that I might win those who are without law. To the weak I became weak, that I might win the weak; I have become all things to all men, so that I may by all means save some. I do all things for the sake of the gospel, so that I may become a fellow partaker of it (1 Corinthians 9:19-23).

This verse is not license to sin, but it speaks to the ability to understand the world while not being slave to its ways. I take this as a call to understand media and the surrounding culture enough to be able to carry a conversation and make connections between the entertainment our society engages for amusement and the Bible which is the power to save all people.

Who Needs to Understand Media?

D o we all need to become media moguls? I do not think so. We first need to start with understanding God has prepared different people for different tasks:

> Now there are varieties of gifts, but the same Spirit. And there are varieties of ministries, and the same Lord. There are varieties of effects, but the same God who works all things in all persons. But to each one is given the manifestation of the Spirit for the common good (1 Corinthians 12:4-7).

We need to find out what task God has for us in the kingdom, and then use the task as a starting point to determine whether we need to understand modern culture as it relates to media entertainment. If we believe we are called to serve in church, Sunday school, children's missions, cleaning and maintaining the church, we may not have a need to understand as fully the media the world produces, but someone called to youth ministry probably does as teenagers inherently seek to entertainment themselves with modern media. People called to international missions, particularly those whom are not western societies do not need to understand the popular arts; but rather focusing on the cultures they are reaching.

If our calling is to our family, workplace, and the people in our western towns, it is best to understand the media culture. Parents particularly need to understand modern pop culture so we can establish appropriate balance with our children: Demanding abstinence from popular media often leads to rebellion, but being passive to what our kids consume will open their heart to more sin than can be imagined.

If our call is to serve local neighborhoods, social programs (like Big Brothers, Big Sisters), community kitchens, and the like, it is also important we can navigate media entertainment so we have the ability to communicate and relate to people we are serving.

In the next sections we will detail specific considerations for evaluating the different formats of media. We will look at videos and movies, music, and video games and how to apply the general tips throughout this book to the different formats of popular entertainment. Refer to the Appendix for a detailed list of the questions and discussion points summarizing the text of the general concepts explained in the preceding chapters.

Understanding Entertainment

U nder the category of cinematic entertainment we will consider movies, television / streaming series, and video channels on online platforms like YouTube. Gaming would be any video games you may buy or stream, while music should obviously be music consumed in any format. We will examine all of the criteria below, some may be more applicable to some forms of media than others, but to a degree, all media entertainment can be evaluated the same way.

Director/Writer

A good starting point is to determine the general reputation of the writer and director of the production. Some directors like Martin Scorsese and Quentin Tarantino have specific reputations of directing films to break down conservative thought. Their *modus operandi* is to create shock value, usually without a moral theme aligning with the Scriptures. Tarentino gave us *Reservoir Dogs*, *Pulp Fiction*, and *Natural Born Killers*. All of which were very influential films, gratuitously violent, and bringing us nothing but unsettling feelings about what we just watched. To contrast these writer/directors, Alex Kendrick has written and directed many films with solid Christian views. Probably his most famous film is *Fireproof*, but my personal favorite was *Facing the Giants*. Both of these films gave us human emotion, temptations, and victory while holding onto a morality in alignment with God's Word.

Other film considerations are *Noah* and *Exodus*. Both of these films are supposedly Biblically based, but to look at the directors, we understand why both films fall short of the mark. Ridley Scott directed *Exodus* and by his own admission, he never even read the part of Exodus the story is based on. He frankly didn't care! We are left with a movie turning Moses into a revolutionary, 'God' being a child, and a totally fabricated story. My main issue with such a film is many people will start assuming the movie follows the Biblical text and will start to believe the movie more than the Biblical account about the events actually unfolding.

But *Exodus* is tame compared to *Noah*. The director, Darren Aronofsky, is an atheist and he actually bragged that the film was "the least biblical biblical film ever made.[95]" Further, Aronofsky is a radical environmentalist and boasts that he made Noah to be the first environmentalist, and those themes seep out of the film. Again, with cinema, most people who watch the movie will start assimilating the film with the stories told in Sunday schools, confusing themselves about what the Bible actually records in Genesis.

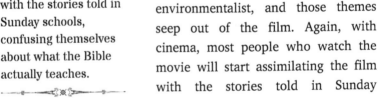

Most people who watch movies will start assimilating the films with the stories told in Sunday schools, confusing themselves about what the Bible actually teaches.

In the music industry, it is important to consider the label, which usually dictates the producers. We talked about Ozzy

Osborne earlier in the book about how he was not the 'prince of darkness' his music portrayed him to be. The record label in control of the first album created and propagated that persona for the shock value in the album debut, and it worked. They were able to pay for some advertisement, but the rest of it came free with the controversy and that alone launched Black Sabbath into the mainstream.

A few decades later, Rawkus records was established to take a risk on known and unknown hip hop artists. They launched some famous talent including Eminem, a controversial rapper known for homophobic lyrics and shock value. Record labels usually specialize in certain types of music and those with similar lyrics and themes. To identify the feel of music from a few artists under that label, one can make an educated guess about the type and content of the music.

So the first principle is to look at the writers, directors, and while we are at it, look to the producers. If they have a general reputation for pushing social agendas, we will find those agendas in the film. If they produce Godly work, expect that. If they merely entertain, than we will likely find just that.

RATING

The rating can tell us some good information, but it is best not to create an absolute decision based on ratings alone. Obviously, with younger children it is probably best to stick with PG or lower, but even then be more cognoscente of what is in the film. Some G rated films over the years have contained a lot of adult themes, which even though such embedded themes will go over the child's head, they may still negatively impact them subconsciously. When our kids get older, we should not hold many absolutes but teach them to read the why behind the restrictions and temper understanding with Biblical reasoning for why some movies are not appropriate to watch. Modern ratings list the reasons why the particular restrictions apply, and I use these reasons as a guiding point. If it contains a lot of nudity or sexuality, I generally stay away. If sexual situations appear in the reasoning, I will look to some parental sections in reviews to determine if the situations are over the top for me or not. Focus on the Family has a more traditional review site for evaluating movies, but many secular review sources are starting to include parental sections as well. We will look at a few of these in the next section.

We need to determine for ourselves and our families what is appropriate for each category. Do we want to restrict all bad language, or are a few instances OK? What about violence? Is violence completely avoided in our home entertainment, or are certain kinds of content allowed? Ultimately, the best thing to do with the ratings is understand how they are assigned and how to read the reasoning behind them, and then train ourselves and our kids to look at the reasons and ask what is appropriate.

I personally have had tremendous results with this approach. I opened up my home on Friday nights for movies with my little in Big Brothers, Big Sisters and let him have friends over. We still had a video rental store in our town and we would go out to look for movies. Even though these kids came from homes which did not regulate the movies they watched, it was great to see the teenager pick up a movie and read the back and put it down saying, "We can't watch this at Tom's house." With enough boundaries and communication, our kids will respect our wishes.

REVIEWS AND CRITICS

M any websites, associations, and companies create reviews for us to read and consider. We need to start like we did with the director: who is the critic? Some critics focus on story lines while others look to cinematic elements, sets, and dialog. The most famous early film critic was not in the United States, but France. André Bazin became known as early as 1943 for his take on realism in the film industry at a time when film often time was used to manipulate reality instead. In other words, he focused more on what could be learned from films based in reality rather than being entertained by films including more super-natural events.

The first critics I remember from my childhood and adolescent years were Siskel and Ebert who were often times on the HBO segments in between movies. Of course, Leonard Maltin was also popular at that time. These secular critics taught us what made a good story, dialog, and plot line. They were succeeded by online critics with independent channels such as The Nostalgia Critic and Cinema Sins. Under the brand of 'edutainment' they sought to bring entertainment to reviews of movies like the YouTube game streamers were doing to the latest video game releases.

These secular critics do little for us in the Christian community because they judge a movie based on the yardstick of popular entertainment rather than in alignment with Biblical truths. Focus on the Family sought to fill that void with Plugged In[96] to demonstrate not only the storyline and themes, but also to show the things many parents may find objectionable in the film from the Christian perspective, or at least, from a 'safe' perspective as would be held in a Christian home. Since the movement of family values (whether or not that is connected to

Christian), more similar, but religiously neutral, sites have also popped up. Kids-in-Mind is a website aimed to give parents more information about what is in a film by categorizing different scenes[97]. This is the best thing, in my opinion, so parents can set the guidelines about what makes a film an appropriate choice. These resources are the best informant of reviews as a Christian because, even though targeted toward parents of kids, they give us an understanding of what is in a film so we can choose whether to watch it or not.

We find similar critics in the video game and music industries. Rolling Stone has been one of the longest standing publications on musical reviews and gossip. Founded in 1967 to focus on music reviews and political reporting, it has been the go-to place for ratings and announcements in the music industry. Plugged In also shifted to add music and video game reviews to its lineup to meet the needs of parents for all popular culture, and these 'parental' reviews will give us as conscientious adults the information we need to evaluate an artist or album.

PUTTING IT ALL TOGETHER

After we have gathered our information about what the producers want us to learn, what the MPAA has rated a film, and some of the content, we now have to evaluate what is good for us, as believers, to watch ourselves, and to allow into our homes. With the information in our hand, we will apply the concepts in Chapter 8 on Examining Everything Carefully. Start here:

> *I will set no worthless thing before my eyes;*
> *I hate the work of those who fall away;*
> *It shall not fasten its grip on me.*
> *(Psalm 101:3)*

If the film is truly worthless, it is best to avoid it. In the terms of this book, worthless may mean the goal is to teach us anything contrary to the teaching in the Bible. If the director is pushing a homosexual agenda like *The Crying Game* or *Torch Song Trilogy*, it is probably best to avoid the film. The Bible does not call us to hate, or be angry toward the homosexual community, but it does teach that the practicing this lifestyle is a sin (*Romans 1:26-27, 1 Corinthians 6:9-11, 1 Timothy 1:8-11*).

Another worthless cinematic would be anything teaching us to engage in sexuality in an immoral way, outside the bounds of marriage. Such franchises as *American Pie, 50 Shades of Grey*, and many others in Hollywood bestow the benefits of such immorality contrary to the clear teaching of Scripture (*1 Corinthians 6:12-20, Colossians 3:5-7, Hebrews 13:4*).

Not all sexuality has to be wrong. I mentioned the movie *Playing for Keeps*, which the main character does engage in immoral sexuality in the beginning of the film, but it is portrayed as having learned a lesson and by the end of the film, he had made a choice to remain faithful, at least on a social level. The lesson learned is worth some value, and the absence of explicit sexual scenes makes the film valid in my view.

Of course, violence follows the same thinking. *Natural Born Killers* did not care to make a lesson by the end of the film, but ended in a possible reality where crime can pay. Piled on top of that was the ultimate theme in the film: violence is fun and gratuitous. To contrast this, the 1994 film *The War* carried some violent themes, depicting some battle scenes from Vietnam but also a fight between two groups of kids which turned into a war between, them complete with tractors, explosions, and blood. This film used the violence to make the point such violence is not worth the price in the end[98]. Similar themes were explored 1983 with *The Outsiders*. In these cases, violence is present in the film, but the first of them teaches us violence for the sake of violence is OK, but the latter two films explore the deep problems with fighting, wars, and differences that extrapolate to hostility.

Language has an interesting rap. The Bible does say not to swear (*Hosea 4:2, James 5:12*). We always, however, need to consider the context. Not to swear in the Bible means not to swear an oath or to deceive someone by saying you swore an oath. Jesus was talking about this very thing in *Matthew 15:3-6*:

> *And He answered and said to them, "Why do you yourselves transgress the commandment of God for the sake of your tradition? For God said, 'HONOR YOUR FATHER AND MOTHER,' and, 'HE WHO SPEAKS EVIL OF FATHER OR MOTHER IS TO BE PUT TO DEATH.' But you say, 'Whoever says to his father or mother, "Whatever I have that would help you has been given to God," he is not to honor his father or his mother.' And by this you invalidated the word of God for the sake of your tradition.*

The context here and in the places the Bible talks about swearing is about oaths, not using profane language as we would define it here. But the reason 'bad' language has such a mark on it in our present world is the meaning behind the words. If you want to drop an F-bomb but see children around so you use the Fr-bomb instead, the meaning is still clear: angry, hateful language used to shock and invoke feelings in the hearer. This falls under two different condemnations in Scripture: Vain language and unprofitable language. For the vain language, Jesus says in *Matthew 12:33-37*:

> *Either make the tree good and its fruit good, or make the tree bad and its fruit bad; for the tree is known by its fruit. You brood of vipers, how can you, being evil, speak what is good? For the mouth speaks out of that which fills the heart. The good man brings out of his good treasure what is good; and the evil man brings out of his evil treasure what is evil. But I tell you*

that every careless word that people speak, they shall give an accounting for it in the day of judgment. For by your words you will be justified, and by your words you will be condemned.

By our words we stand or fall. Angry, hateful, shocking words point to a heart full of anger and strife. These angry words are called idle words, and bear with them condemnation. When these words are the hero's expression in media, it will start to impact us in such a way we could subconsciously start emulating the way of speech. To this end, a high school friend and I were determined people who swore a lot were generally people who were not as successful, and so we wanted to live without vulgarity and we did for quite a long while. But eventually I started getting into Warren G and 2 Pac and the obscenities in their music began to infiltrate my heart. By the time Jesus plucked me as a brand from the fire I was cussing like a dirty sailor at every turn. That is the outstretching of the way such words can impact us. Overall, I am not saying to avoid a movie, song, or game that has a few bad words, but be careful that if that character is the hero in the production, you may start to gravitate toward similar speech.

The second, unprofitable language, is best summed up by Paul in *Ephesians 4:29*:

Let no unwholesome word proceed from your mouth, but only such a word as is good for edification according to the need of the moment, so that it will give grace to those who hear.

Unprofitable is not the same as vain words, but they can overlap. I first began to understand this verse when I attended a Bible study which started teaching theologically void church growth materials. The book we were reading started talking about this verse from Ephesians, and it turns out, the empty hearts of the men in that group started using *Ephesians 4:29* as a meme for the rest of the night, using the very verse as an insult, to put people down. Needless to say, this was the last time I have ever stepped foot into the group. In a similar thread, we see people taking benign words and twisting them as an insult. This was the theme in an Adventures in Odyssey episode called *War of the Words*[99] to explain this very phenomenon. Eugene and Connie are in an argument as usual and Eugene, in character, uses a word above everyone's head. While the word fit the situation, it also became a meme used as an insult by the kids in the episode. Such is the heart of unprofitable language: anything used as a put down, rather than building up. This means it may not be a 'swear' word as we define them, but the heart of the matter is to hurt someone else.

Consider the words, phrases, and most importantly, the heart behind the language in the media you consume. Make a solid determination of the types of language and spirit allowed in your mind and your family's entertainment and seek out that which is good.

CONCLUDING REMARKS

I set out in writing this book with a multi-tier purpose. First, it is written to younger believers who are finding their way in our crazy world. My prayer for you is the words in this book and the lessons from the stars, both living and dead, will be a warning about the importance of living your life for Christ. As Kirk Cameron is often asked if he is missing some of the 'fun' in Hollywood for living like a Christian, he has replied that his old colleagues' fun often left them six feet under. He co-starred roles with Corey Haim who is dead of a drug overdose. He auditioned parts with River Phoenix, who is dead also of an overdose. Cameron also points to the often empty lives of his former co-stars and asks what fun is he really missing? Let this be a lesson to you young people: Following the ways of Jesus Christ will lead to a better, more fulfilling life.

To the parents reading this book, I pray you may understand the dangers popular media culture may present to your children. But also, I pray you will find the lessons about talking to your kids more important than merely restricting access to musicians, television shows, and video games. This is worth a conversation, and analysis of the Scriptures, and an honest review of the entertainment your children want to see. Do not merely restrict, but also do not blindly allow, for the message the media man wants to teach your children is not for their benefit. Have the hard conversations and learn what media your children are consuming, and use that as a springboard for conversation.

To the pastors and teachers, I hope you will see that blindly consuming entertainment to relate with your flock is not a means to reach your congregation, but neither is complete absence. Stuart McAllister wisely said our modern culture speaks the language of popular entertainment. If you are completely ignorant of such entertainment you may not be able to relate to your parishioners, but if you only speak that language you will become so worldly as to be rendered ineffective in preaching the Gospel. Instead, learn to know what is out there, and make the connections back to the Bible to draw your flock back to the written word of the Good Shepherd.

No matter who you are, I pray you will find the Scripture and guidance in this book useful for analyzing any media you may encounter whether it be a movie or television show, a video game, or some music from a new artist. Remember to always examine everything carefully. Hold fast to that which is good, and abstain from every evil thing.

CHAPTER QUESTIONS

1. Do you serve in a capacity that merits more understanding of the popular arts?

2. Does your church fall into one of the two errors?

3. What resources do you use for evaluating media?

APPENDIX 1

THE MEDIA DETOX

When I became a Christian, I had a lot of work to do in my soul. The movies full of sexual immorality and senseless gore will be forever in my head and heart seeking a foothold to express themselves. My teenage years of evil music, complete with pentagrams, Satanic symbols, vulgarity, sexual references are likewise forever in my head. It is these images which attack my spirit as I pray and torment my soul to tears as I think of the years of my life squandered by such filth. I cannot get those back, but I can move forward with better decisions, better input, and by crowding out the evil with the power and light of God. This is my 'detox' plan. I assure if you are likewise tormented by your past media input, it gets easier to resist the thoughts.

1. Stop the flow of negative media immediately. Once we identify a program or video game as bad input, cut it off from further influence (*1 Thessalonians 5:21-22*). David likewise said, "*I will set no worthless thing before my eyes (Psalm 101:3).*

2. Replace the bad with good. If we do not immediately fill the void left by removing a movie, band, or game from our life, we will go back to that old source of entertainment, but each cycle we make becomes harder to overcome next time (*Matthew 12:43-45*). I am not suggesting we remove all non-Christian material from our life, just to abstain from clearly evil in the things we use as entertainment.

3. Purify our minds with the Word. *Romans 12* reminds us to transform ourselves by the renewing of our mind. In

Ephesians 4-5, Paul contrasts how we are to live in the Spirit as contrasted to our natural state.

4. Stand firm against evil. Paul writes in *Ephesians 6:10-17* about putting on the full armor of God. Several components of standing firm are mentioned. Ultimately, Paul writes that our true battle is with spiritual forces, not our own flesh (*Ephesians 6:12*). We need to be armed with Truth which is knowing what in our world is really right. Without Truth, we move toward the wrong goal. Righteousness is living correctly so we are both an example, and blessed by God. The Gospel gives us hope for others, and our Faith allows us to make good decisions even when it seems all things are not right in the world. Salvation ushers us into the Kingdom of Heaven, and the Word of God is our ultimate weapon for life.

Coming to Christ as an adult gave me perspective of the sin which contaminated me. James reminds us to be unstained by the world (*James 1:27*). Whether we have been Christians for a few days or several decades, we always need to examine our life and entertainment carefully. We need to prevent evil from entering our minds and work hard to clean up the mess created when it does get in. These steps can help us follow Christ more in our culture.

APPENDIX 2

QUESTIONS TO EVALUATE MEDIA ENTERTAINMENT

The following questions are designed to get you thinking about media entertainment in your life. They are not meant to suggest the mere presence of certain content immediately vilifies your entertainment choices. Taking together with the call to be objective about what we consume, these questions are just to get you thinking about the task ahead.

MOVIES / TELEVISION / STREAMING

- What is the reputation of the writer, director, and producer?

- Are the actors active in social causes? Are those causes worthy or not?

- What is the basic story line about? Does it ultimately teach a lesson worth learning?

- Is the main 'hero' a good or bad character?

- Do we even know what good and bad means in the context of the film?

- Are the vulgar scenes explicit or do they portray sin without being graphic?

- Is there unnecessary language not adding to the production?

- Do the main characters grow in their moral conduct?

- Do they mention the Bible / Christians? In what light?

MUSIC

- What is reputation of the artist and producer?

- Do the lyrics teach a concept? Is it a lesson worth learning?

- Do the songs glorify sin? (Note the mere mention of sin does not mean glorification)

- Is the artist humble in life?

- Is there unnecessary language that does not add to the production?

- Does the production mention the Bible / Christians? In what light?

VIDEO GAMES

- What is the reputation of the game author / producers?

- Does the game tell a story line? Is it a lesson worth learning?

- Does the game have the player engaging in clear acts of sin?

- Is the character good or bad? Do we know what good or bad means in the context of the game?

- Is there unnecessary language that does not add to the production?

- Do the main characters grow in their moral conduct?

- Do they mention the Bible / Christians? In what light?

BIBLIOGRAPHY

1. The Last Roman "Triumph", *Foxes Book of Martyrs*, John Foxe, Chapter 3
2. Pompii, *All This Bad Blood*, 2013, Bastille, Virgin Records
3. U.S.C Breaks Ground for a Film-TV School, *New York Times*, November 25, 1981
4. ibid
5. *What Ever Happened to Right and Wrong*, Chip Ingram, Living on the Edge
6. *Decadence: Decline of the Western World*, Pria Viswalingam, 2011, Fork Films
7. *The Closing of the American Mind*, Allan Bloom, 1987, Touchstone Publishing, Part 1; Music
8. The real effect of make-believe Don't let filmmakers tell you they can't shape public opinion, *Atlanta Journal Constitution*, May 19th, 1991 pg D1
9. Hayes Code, http://pre-code.com/the-motion-picture-production-code-of-1930/, Accessed November 11, 2018
10. Confessions of a Hollywood Propagandist, Nancy Snow, https://learcenter.org/publication/warners-war-confessions-of-a-hollywood-propagandist-harry-warner-fdr-and-celluloid-persuasion/, Accessed November 11, 2018
11. *Advertising by the Federal Government: An Overview*, Kevin R. Kosar, Congressional Research Service
12. *Cult of the Suicide Bomber*, 2006, Disinformation Studios
13. MTV is Rock Around the Clock, *Philadelphia Inquirer*, Nov 3, 1982
14. 2000 Michael Greene Grammy Music Awards speech, https://www.youtube.com/watch?v=-Glq-ecgGjE, Accessed November 11, 2018
15. 2001 Michael Greene Grammy Music Awards Speech, https://www.youtube.com/watch?v=FP4vcVcydkM, Accessed November 11, 2018
16. Ibid
17. Columbine: Whose Fault Is It, *Rolling Stone*, May 28, 1999
18. Heavy metal and violence: More than a myth?, *CNN*, May 12, 2008
19. Six Most Idiotic Attempts to Blame Musicians for Violent Events (or, the Tucson Tragedy was Caused by a Crazy Person, Not by Drowning Pool's "Bodies Hit the Floor", *LA Weekly*, Thursday, January 13, 2011
20. *Deadly Lessons, Understanding Lethal School Violence*, The National Academy Press, 2003
21. Heavy metal and violence: More than a myth?, *CNN*, May 12, 2008

22. Extreme Metal Music and Anger Processing, *Frontiers in Human Neuroscience*, 21 May 2015, Article 272

23. Exposure to Violent Media: The Effects of Songs with Violent Lyrics on Aggressive Thoughts and Feelings, *Journal of Personality and Social Psychology*, 2003, Vol 84, No 5, 960-971

24. *Media Violence and Children*, Douglas Gentile, 2003, Praeger, Advances in Applied Developmental Psychology (Book 22)

25. *Riders on the Storm*, John Densmore, 1990, Delta Music Biographies, Bantam Doubleday Dell Publishing, Chapter 7

26. On MC5 and the Evolution of Pop Music, YouTube, https://www.youtube.com/watch?v=6qgSBrgZlzM, Accessed November 11, 2018

27. Video Game Effects – Confirmed, Suspected, and Speculative, *Simulation and Gaming*, Vol 40, No 3, June 2009, pg 377-403

28. Columbine: Whose fault is it?, *Rolling Stone*, May 28, 1999

29. Pumped up Kicks, *Torches*, 2010, Foster the People, Columbia Records

30. 'Pumped up kicks' Yanked from L.A. Airwaves After Newtown Massacre, *TMZ*, December 19, 2012

31. *Bowling for Columbine*, Michael Moore, 2002, Alliance Atlantis Communications Inc

32. Columbine: Whose Fault Is It?, *Rolling Stone*, May 28, 1999

33. MTV is Rock Around the Clock, *Philadelphia Inquirer*, Nov 3, 1982

34. *Dancing in the Dark*, Schultze, *et. al.*, 1991, Wm B Eerdmans Publishing, Chapter 7

35. *A Long Hard Road Out of Hell*, Marilyn Manson, 1998, Regan Books, Chapter 6

36. Ibid, Chapter 11

37. Ibid, Chapter 6

38. Ibid

39. *Chant and Be Happy: The Power of Mantra Meditation*, A C Bhaktivedanta Swami Prabhupada, 1992, The Bhaktivedanta Book Trust, Preface by George Harrison

40. Ibid, Chapter 1

41. Ibid

42. Ibid

43. Ibid

44. Ibid

45. Tears of a Clown: The American Nightmare That Created the Insane Clown Posse, *The Vice*, April 30, 2015

46. Violent J Breaks Down Insane Clown Posse's 'Joker Card' Box Set, *Rolling Stone*, February 13, 2015

47. Ibid

48. Thy Unveiling, *The Wraith: Shangri-La*, 2002, Insane Clown Posse, Psychopathic Records

49. Tears of a Clown: The American Nightmare That Created the Insane Clown Posse, *The Vice*, April 30, 2015

50. To Catch a Predator, *Bang! Pow! Boom!*, 2009, Insane Clown Posse, Psychopathic Records

51. Piggy Pie, *The Great Milenko*, 1997, Insane Clown Posse, Psychopathic Records

52. Tears of a Clown: The American Nightmare That Created the Insane Clown Posse, *The Vice*, April 30, 2015

53. Gangta's Paradise, *Gangsta's Paradise*, 1995, Coolie, Tommy Boy Records

54. *Alice Cooper and Alcohol*, https://www.youtube.com/watch?v=dvzao_6dBYA, Accessed November 19, 2018

55. *I Am Ozzy*, Ozzy Osbourne, 2009, Grand Central Publishing

56. *The Heroine Diaries*, Nikki Sixx, 2007, Pocket Books

57. Not Afraid, *Recovery*, 2010, Eminem, Interscope Records

58. *I Am Ozzy*, Ozzy Osbourne, 2009, Grand Central Publishing

59. *Unashamed*, Lecrae Moore, 2016, B&H Publishing Group

60. Ibid, Chapter 1

61. Soaring Sales Make Wayfarers Anything but a Risky Business, *Los Angeles Times*, August 7, 1988

62. Test for Echo, *Test for Echo*, 1996, Rush, Atlantic Records

63. Director's Commentary on *Office Space*, Mike Judge, 1999, Fox

64. *Save me From Myself*, Brian 'Head' Welch, 2007, Harper One

65. *Iron Man: My Journey through Heaven and Hell with Black Sabbath*, Tony Iommi, 2012, Da Capo Press

66. Kirk Cameron: I'll only kiss my wife, *Today*, October 14, 2016

67. Hero, *Awake*, 2009, Skillet, Lava Records

68. *Media: Friend or Foe?*, Stuart McAllister, 2006, RZIM

69. Quoted from an old CD: Swing the Bat, John Maxwell released by Goad International, though I cannot find any reference to this resource, but a few soundcloud accounts do have the original 'Swing the Bat' production

70. *Media: Friend or Foe?*, Stuart McAllister, 2006, RZIM

71. *Media: Friend or Foe?*, Stuart McAllister, 2006, RZIM

72. *Confessions*, Saint Augustine, VI-9-24

73. Book 1 Chapter 8, *Foundations of the Christian Faith*, James Montgomery Boice, 1986, Intervarsity Press,

74. video-game-addiction.org, a new defunct website. Archive at https://web.archive.org/web/20161219225330/http://video-game-addiction.org/, Accessed November 11, 2018

75. Summarized from video-game-addiction.org, a new defunct website. Archive at https://web.archive.org/web/20161219225330/http://video-game-addiction.org/, Accessed November 11, 2018

76. *Forget big change, start with a tiny habit: BJ Fogg at TEDxFremont*, https://www.youtube.com/watch?v=AdKUJxjn-R8, Accessed January, 12, 2019

77. *Testing and Temptations: A Guide to Sanctification*, Thomas Murosky, 2018, Our Walk in Christ Publishing

78. Prize fighting and the Birth of Movie Censorship, Barak Y. Orbach, 2009, *Yale Journal of Law & the Humanities*, Vol 21, Issue 2, Article 3

79. Eat Me Alive, *Defenders of the Faith*, 1986, Judas Priest, Columbia

80. 7 Words You Can Never Say on Television, *Class Clown*, 1972, George Carlin, Little David / Atlantic Records

81. *Kids*, Larry Clark, 1995, Shining Excalibur Films

82. *The Crying Game*, Neil Jordan, 1992, Palace Pictures

83. *Exodus: Gods and Kings*, Ridley Scott, 2014, Chernin Entertainment

84. *American Pie*, Paul Weitz and Chris Weitz, 1999, Zide/Perry Productions

85. *Lucifer*, Tom Kapinos, Since January 25, 2016, Fox

86. *Family Guy*, Seth MacFarlane, Since January 31, 1999, Fox

87. *Playing For Keeps*, Gabriele Muccino, 2012, Nu Image Productions

88. *Simon Birch*, Mark Steven Johnson, 1998, Hollywood Productions

89. *Fight Club*, David Fincher, 1999, Fox 2000 Pictures

90. *The Devil*, 2010, John Erick Dowdle, Media Rights Capital

91. *The Book of Eli*, The Hughes Brothers, 2010, Alcon Entertainment

92. *The Passion of the Christ*, Mel Gibson, 2004, Icon Productions

93. *God's Word and Your Spiritual Growth*, John MacArthur, Grace to you, GTY98

94. *The Screwtape Letters*, C.S. Lewis, 1961, Geoffrey Bles Publishing, Chapter 12

95. Darren Aronofsky Calls 'Noah' The 'Least Biblical Film Ever Made', *Huffington Post*, March 11, 2014

96. www.pluggedin.com, a media review website run by Focus on the Family

97. kids-in-mind.com, a media review website that is secular in focus geared toward better parental decisions in media entertainment

98. *The War*, Jon Avnet, 1994, Universal Pictures

99. War of the Words, *A Journey of Choices*, Adventures in Odyssey, Episode 265, Volume 20, 2004, Focus on the Family, Tyndale Entertainment

SCRIPTURE INDEX

Made in the USA
San Bernardino, CA
16 May 2020

71893281R00122